Acclaim for

An absolute must for anyone who is buying or selling a home!
Highly recommended.

–Susan Levitt, *Taoist Feng Shui, Taoist Astrology* and *Teen Feng Shui*

Feng Shui for Real Estate is the perfect resource for buying
or selling your next home. This book is filled with practical
and detailed recommendations to make simple yet effective
changes for your situation. A wise investment as your guide
for one of the major decisions in your life..

–Master RD Chin, feng shui architect and author, *Feng Shui Revealed*
and *Sitting at the Edge of Floating Moon*

A detailed, easy-to-understand feng shui guide for anyone
buying or selling property This informative book will ensure
harmony and happiness in any new home.

–Sarah Bartlett, *Feng Shui Plain and Simple* and *Feng Shui for Lovers*

Clear Englebert is very knowledgeable about feng shui
and explains the importance of the placements well.
I highly recommend his feng shui books.

–Clarence Lau, traditional feng shui master

Another wonderful feng shui book from Clear, filled with so much
valuable information! If you are looking for a new home, I suggest
you take the time to read all the detailed information he provides,
along with a variety of feng shui cures to help you if you happen
to fall in love with a house that has less-than-perfect feng shui!

–Rodika Tchi, *Feng Shui for Healing* and *The Healing Power of Smudging*

FENG SHUI
for
REAL
ESTATE

FENG SHUI
for
REAL
ESTATE

A GUIDE FOR BUYERS, SELLERS AND AGENTS

CLEAR ENGLEBERT

WATERMARK
PUBLISHING

ISBN 978-1-948011-60-0 (print edition)
ISBN 978-1-948011-61-7 (e-book edition)

Library of Congress Control Number: 2021942894

Book Design & Production
Dawn Sakamoto Paiva

Watermark Publishing
1000 Bishop St., Suite 806
Honolulu, HI 96813
Telephone 1-808-587-7766
Toll-free 1-866-900-BOOK
sales@bookshawaii.net
www.bookshawaii.net

Printed in the United States

Contents

Introduction

This is my seventh feng shui book. My other books have flowed nicely from topic to topic, but not this book. It jumps from topic to topic because the information is arranged based on the *severity of the problem*. It's written for a very specific purpose—to be a feng shui guide during a real estate transaction.

Feng shui is the Chinese art of placement—where a building is placed within the landscape and how objects are placed within the building. Feng shui instructs us how to maximize the flow of prosperity, harmony, and health. Its roots go back six thousand years, but the general principles can be applied to modern situations. The home (or workplace) you select can influence what happens in your life.

The feng shui in this book is from the **Form School**, which I feel is best adapted for the West. Form School, sometimes called Landform, is the oldest kind of feng shui. It is distinct from Compass School feng shui, which uses astrology and numerology.

Feng shui uses a language of symbols to help you reach your goals quickly without spinning your wheels. It shows how to remove symbolic obstacles from your environment. Fewer symbolic obstacles translate to fewer real obstacles in your life. If you don't believe me, just try it. That's how I became convinced. Feng shui is not difficult, because it mostly aligns with common sense. I continue to hear from my clients: "Everything you've said makes sense to me."

The use of Chinese terminology, such as chi, can be mystifying. Chi is energy in any form. People's life energy is chi. *Attracting* chi is the same as attracting a person's

xii FENG SHUI FOR REAL ESTATE

attention. *Guiding* chi is the same as making a destination obvious and easy to get to. *Manipulating* chi energy (that's feng shui) involves observation and a few simple rules. Your intuition is your strongest guide; don't ignore it.

My feng shui practice does not involve lucky numbers or lucky directions or lucky objects. I firmly believe in *strong* houses—symbolically powerful as well as physically sturdy. They empower you immeasurably. Ideally, a home should support everyday life, making it easy to be organized and comfortable.

Feng shui's premise is this: The spaces where we spend the greatest amount of our time influence our lives the most.

Remedies

When a situation needs improvement, I recommend two kinds of adjustments: **real** and **symbolic**. I call them remedies; they are also called solutions, cures, or fixes. A real remedy changes the situation so that the problem doesn't exist anymore. When a real remedy isn't feasible, use a symbolic remedy. It symbolizes a change, and you are thereby doing the best you can under the circumstances.

If you are using a symbolic remedy, you can make it stronger by expressing your intention. *Say out loud, at the moment that you do it,* **why** you are doing it. The *power of your voice* is significant in this instance. State your intention, using your own words. The rationales associated with particular remedies are explained in this book. It's important to know how subtle environmental energy affects us.

Pick the remedy or remedies that are most feasible or make sensible in your particular situation. Keep with your own style. I urge you: don't make your home tacky or awkward in the name of feng shui. I've certainly seen that happen. Listen to your intuition and common sense. Ugly remedies may work, but a thoughtful remedy that blends with your style works *so much better.*

PART ONE

FOR BUYERS

Advice for Buyers

The original use of feng shui was to select auspicious property, and that's still the best use of feng shui. Why pay good money for problematic property when you can be aware of what to avoid and what to look for? Selecting a new home is one of the most important decisions of your life. It can be as important as selecting who you're going to marry.

This book will guide you through the most crucial aspects of selecting your home. This same advice is applicable for buyers and renters, although renters don't always have the flexibility to execute some of the remedies.

Truth be told, if you're living in a home that has major feng shui problems, it's good you're holding this book. You'll need it! Otherwise, you might easily end up with even more feng shui problems in your next home. A problematic home creates muddled thinking that won't get you into a fine new home. Likewise, people in an energetically great home will usually pick that same energy for their next home. They're already used to supportive energy and better able to notice its presence in a prospective next home.

It is doubtful that a feng shui–friendly house will be the cheapest one in the neighborhood. The cheapest houses are probably rife with feng shui problems. When feng shui–friendly houses show up on the market, they tend to sell for at least what the seller is asking because if the seller is living in the home they are in a strong position.

The information that follows is organized by the severity of a problem or the importance of a good feature. Some things are much more important than others, so the most crucial items are covered first, then the less important, on down to lists of "things that would be nice to have" in the new space. You may not be able to pick a home that satisfies *all* the criteria for a feng shui–friendly house. Multiple remedies are given for the problems that are noted. It's ideal if the house doesn't have a problem in the first place, but many homes do.

This book is based on my own years of experience of noticing which feng shui problems are most severe and matter most when selecting a new home. There are a few problems that are so severe that I sincerely advise not purchasing that home. In those cases, if you wait to find a more ideal home, you will reap happy rewards for years to come.

Condominiums

Much of the advice for buyers concerns only free-standing homes. If you are buying a condominium, the sections that most concern you are:

- Electromagnetic Fields, page 8
- Under Airplane Flight Path, page 9
- Missing Back Corners, page 9
- Central Bathroom, page 11
- Stairs in Line with Front Door, page 18
- Spiral Staircases, page 26

If the potential new condo has any of the above problems, don't buy it. Don't compromise—wait for a better place to show up. A better place *will* show up. You'll recognize it when you see it, and you'll be very glad you waited.

Once you've ruled out those severe problems, use the sections of this book that are about *interiors*. Those sections start on these pages:

- Extremely Important Issues, page 26
- Of Moderate Importance, page 32
- Nice to Have, page 45
- Other Considerations, page 55

Renters

Apartment Rentals

Follow the advice under the previous section, Condominiums, page 3.

House Rentals

Follow the advice for buyers, beginning on page 2.

The Most Profound Problems

My strongest advice is to avoid buying buildings that have the profound problems listed in this chapter. These situations are too severe. Even with remedies, a problem often lingers. There are homes that shouldn't have been built in a certain way, or at a particular location. Just because somebody built it doesn't mean you should live there. Problems in any other category can be successfully fixed with remedies. These are the few instances where I would tell a client, "No, don't buy this home." Except for the bathroom locations, these instances are all somewhat rare.

Very often, homes with these problems will have more "affordable" prices. Well, that could be because the people who are living there are having problems *achieving their goals*. In my experience, it's not to be expected that homes with really good feng shui will be sold at rock-bottom prices. Homes with good feng shui are more likely to experience a bidding war when the property is for sale.

If, after all my words of warning, you are still tempted to buy a home with one of these "Most Profound Problems," you need to do a mental evaluation. Go inside your mind and find that switch that is currently turned toward "I want it. I love it." Move that switch to "I'll wait. I'll trust and wait." Only you can find that switch, and don't fool yourself into thinking that you can't find it. It's always there, and it may feel painful when you move the switch. It's a strong, conscious act of will and it will move you toward future happiness.

Exterior

Severe Landform

Symbols of protection are probably the oldest and most powerful symbols in feng shui. The landform around the house says either "protected and backed" or "exposed and vulnerable."

A building is vulnerable if the land behind it severely slopes down. Look for property on the other side of the road. A house is strengthened by having land rise behind it, unless the slope is too steep, such as a nearby cliff.

A location is too exposed (and thereby symbolically vulnerable) if it is:

- on a hilltop with all sides exposed, and the land slopes downward all around the house
- beside the ocean, with no buffering vegetation between the house and the ocean

Remedies

Remedies for bad landform begin on page 20. If the slope or exposure is severe, the remedies will be much less effective. Avoiding severely bad landform is much better than trying to remedy it.

Triangular Lot

Regularly shaped lots (four sides in either a square or a rectangle) are preferred for a balanced life. Any lot with a very bizarrely shaped map outline is not advisable. Triangular lots are the most extreme, having only three sides. The message is that something is likely to be missing in your life. The very worst triangular shape is one with a tight acute angle. (See Illustration 1.) The worst scenario is when the front door faces directly toward a tight, narrow corner of the lot. It suggests that things could get tighter for you in the future. The larger a lot is, the less of a problem its triangular shape is.

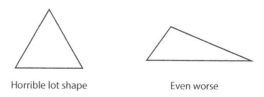

Horrible lot shape   Even worse

Illustration 1: Triangle lot

If the property will only be used commercially, a triangular lot is not likely to be a problem. The busy yang nature of commercial use can overcome bad lot shape. If the lot contains multiple apartments or condominiums, it is almost certainly not a problem. The unit you live in is yours, but the lot is not.

Remedies

Lights, mirrors, and good landscaping are your choices.

• Use plantings to shape the tight corners of the lot to give the impression that it is more square.

• Put mirrors (small ones are less obtrusive and usually more appropriate) at the edge of your property, near the corners, facing into your property. They symbolically expand the property.

• Light up any tight corners on your lot to symbolically expand them. Solar lights are fine if they receive enough sun. Lights on poles are preferred, but any light is a huge improvement over no light in this situation. This solution takes an ongoing commitment on your part because the lights must be kept functional and turned on at least occasionally.

• If the front door faces a tight corner, put a mirror outside the front door, facing away from the house. A bagua mirror (see Glossary) would be best. The mirror pushes the tight energy away from the home.

Electromagnetic Fields

This is a rarity, but very important. Don't live or work on a site that has strong electromagnetic fields (EMFs). Those sites are usually located:

• right next to an electric substation

• close to high cross-country electric lines

• in a building where the regular municipal electric lines (and especially transformers) are within fifteen feet of the structure

• in a unit that is *directly above* a room with all the electric power boxes for a multistory building

In any of these instances, you should check the fields with a gaussmeter (which checks magnetism) before purchasing the property. I've seen some gaussmeters offered on Amazon fairly cheaply. Mine is a Trifield meter from Alphalab—it's the same device that cardiologists use (see Retail Sources, page 136).

Even if you've never heard of EMFs until now, learn about them. There's plenty of documentation on strong EMFs and health problems (see Recommended Reading, page 72). The old feng shui masters didn't use a gaussmeter because strong EMFs didn't exist back then. But they do exist in certain instances of modern life, and it's best to avoid frequent exposures to high levels.

Remedy

Don't try to remedy this problem with devices. EMFs can be blocked only by thick, solid metal. (To be completely correct, I should say that a metal grid will work, if sized according to the frequency of concern.) If the EMFs are strong, don't live there.

Under Low Airplane Flight Path

A home that is directly under low-flying aircraft can never support solid rest. Locations that are very near the take-off and landing of loud machines in the air do not qualify as true home sites.

Remedy

There is no remedy that can truly restore peace to a home that is disturbed by the sounds of low-flying aircraft. Don't bother looking at homes that are under low airplane flight paths—don't even consider them.

Interior

Missing Back Corners

The best shape for the outline of a building, as seen from above, is a square or rectangle. The regularity of the shape suggests less chaos and that events will occur at a manageable pace. One of the worst shapes is an outline with either of the two back corners missing. The back corners are the *power corners*. When a person is in one of those corners, they can face toward the home's front entrance, while their back is covered (symbolizing support) by the home's corner. Illustrations 2 and 3 show examples of missing back corners.

If the far-right back corner (Relationship Area) is missing, relationships will probably not be satisfactory, and if the far-left back corner (Wealth Area) is missing there will likely be money problems.

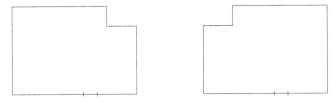

Illustrations 2 & 3: Missing back corners

I've been to only one house where the floor plan was a triangle with only three corners. I told the young couple to move, and they did. They then found the house of their dreams on property with more room for their children to play outside. The best homes have floor plans with four corners—definitely no less, and hopefully no more. A home with only three corners most definitely has something missing.

Remedies

Go outside to the place where the two walls would meet if the corner were not missing. (That's Point A on Illustrations 4 and 5.) Place objects at those points to energetically claim the space as part of the inside of the home. For a missing left corner put a valuable object, and for a missing right corner put two equal objects. People often use coins because they can be buried in the ground and are unnoticeable.

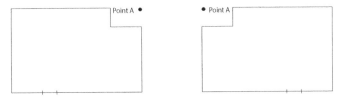

Illustrations 4 & 5: Remedying a missing corner outside the home

The other remedy is applied inside the home. Put mirrors on one or both of the two walls that are tangent to the missing area. (See Illustrations 6 and 7.) Say out loud that you are symbolically increasing the size of the home. The mirrors can be as small as a dime and the reflective side should face into the room. The mirrors can be hidden behind artwork.

Right corner with mirrors   Left corner with mirrors

Illustrations 6 & 7: Remedying a missing corner inside the home

Central Bathroom

Bathrooms are the most problematic rooms in the house. They earn this designation by having three strikes against them.

• They are dominated by fixtures with Water and have no Fire appliances to balance them. In comparison, kitchens have both Fire and Water (fixtures and appliances) and are therefore balanced.

• Bathrooms have two or three drains, and often more. Drains symbolize good fortune/wealth leaving.

• Bathrooms are for the elimination of body waste. For most of humanity's history, we've "done our business" somewhere outside of the walls of the home. Bringing a room for waste elimination into the walls of the home is a radical departure from thousands of years of outhouses.

The location of the bathroom (or bathrooms) is the first thing I look at when someone asks me to look at the floor plan of a home that they're considering moving into. If any bathroom does not touch an outside wall of the house or unit, I always say no. Bathrooms that don't touch an outside wall are referred to as central (or center) bathrooms. They portend disease, divorce, bankruptcy, or death—and sometimes all four things in one house! (See Illustration 8.)

Illustration 8:
A center bathroom does
not have to be in the
center of the building.
It only needs to be
surrounded by the interior
of the home on all sides.

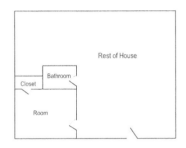

In a condo or apartment, the bathroom is fine as long as it touches a wall that is tangent to a space that is not in your unit. (See Illustration 9.)

Illustration 9:
These bathroom locations
are not a problem.

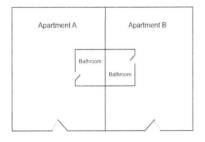

The bathroom does not need to have a tub or shower to be a center bathroom. If there's a toilet, it is considered a bathroom. Be watchful of powder rooms under stairs. If that bathroom doesn't touch an outside wall, it is a center bathroom.

The most energetically healthy bathrooms have functional windows to the outside. The window can be on any wall in the room. (See Illustration 10.)

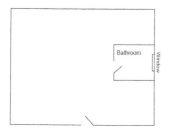

Illustration 10: A healthy bathroom. At least one side is tangent to an outside wall, preferably with a window.

A center bathroom with a skylight is still a center bathroom.

I realize that some feng shui authors are not as "hard line" on center bathrooms as I am. Only once in my career have I seen a center bathroom that wasn't a big problem. In that case, the home had an extremely powerful natural landform surrounding it.

I know quite a few homes are now being built with center bathrooms. Luckily, they're still in the minority. Please heed this advice and shop elsewhere. Don't pay good money for a big problem. Buy a different home.

Remedies

The only real remedy is not feasible for most people: remove the bathroom. Like all real remedies it really does completely solve the problem. Symbolic remedies can never quite achieve that.

The first two remedies below are specific for center bathrooms. The others will greatly improve the vibration of any bathroom.

• If there is another bathroom, **use the center bathroom less**.

• Put **mirrors on two adjacent walls** inside the bathroom. The silvering on the backs of the mirrors is a symbolic *sealing agent*—keeping the body waste energy away from the rest of the house. Never put mirrors on opposite walls where one mirror can be seen directly across from the other mirror. Mirrors on adjacent walls are never a problem, even if the two mirrors meet in a corner. I discuss opposite mirrors on page 63.

• Put a **bagua mirror** outside the bathroom door, *above* the door—not *on* the door. Its purpose is to symbolically reflect the energy of the rest of the house away from this bathroom.

• **Keep the door closed** when someone isn't coming or going. Use a self-closing hinge if necessary.

• Put a **full-length mirror on the outside** of the bathroom door. Its purpose is to symbolically "erase" the bathroom. It does this by showing the hallway in the mirror instead of the bathroom. It is also a sealing agent.

• The **toilet lid should always be down** when not in use. I recommend toilet lids that gently close themselves.

• Hang a **tiny wind chime** inside the bathroom so that when the bathroom door is opened about four inches, the top of the door lightly touches the bottom of the wind chime. The purpose is to lift the energy that enters the bathroom. The wind chime cure won't work for bathrooms with sliding doors or with doors that reach the ceiling. Doors of that height are not uncommon in condos. In that case, use a well-tuned door harp. They are readily found online. Never use bells that clang directly against a door.

- Put a **heavy weight,** such as a flat barbell weight, directly under the sink drain (if that area is in a cabinet). The weight acts as a grounding symbol to counter the flush vibration. It's heavy and solid and couldn't possibly get flushed. Weights symbolize mountains that will not erode. They're going to stay where placed!

All the following remedies relate to the Chinese teaching of the Five Elements. It's an ancient cosmological theory and is not most modern people's worldview. Fortunately, you don't need that worldview to use the remedies. For a more in-depth discussion, see page 99 of the "For Sellers" section. It explains the bagua and the Five Element theory. You don't need to know the background to know the application, so here, quickly, is the application:

- The plant **Sansevieria** (snake plant or mother-in-law's tongue) can be used effectively around the toilet or drain. Its strong uprising form (almost like flames) very effectively says "no" to that down-and-out flush vibration. Place it in pots on the floor on one or both sides of the toilet tank. Alternately, a single pot could be placed (securely) on the top of the toilet tank. I like a Sansevieria called Bantel's Sensation which has unusually bright white variegation, doesn't get very big, and is a bit uncommon. It looks charming, distinctive, and unexpected in a bathroom.

- Wet is yin; dry and fire are yang. Bathrooms are too yin. *Complicated* is also a yin trait, while *simple* is yang. Therefore, **restrained decorating** helps to balance the yin/yang energy.

- Make any shade of **green or yellow** the theme color of the bathroom. Keep it to one color for simplicity but make it any shade you like. Green represents the feng shui Element Wood (a yang element), and yellow represents Earth, which can control Water, like an earth dam can control a reservoir of water. (See Elements in the Glossary, page 134.)

• If a pattern (in fabric, wallpaper, or other items) is used in the bathroom, **plant imagery** is preferred. That's because plants suck up water to build their plant bodies. Their image symbolically drains excess water in the bathroom. Plant pictures are good in bathrooms, as well as items made of plants, such as wood or bamboo.

• Real **plants are ideal in bathrooms**. I've discussed Sansevieria, but any growing plant is great. Artificial plants are also fine in bathrooms. They represent living plants, and just need to be kept clean. They're certainly easier than trying to keep a real plant alive in a windowless bathroom. Don't keep dried plants in a bathroom (or any room). They're dead and they represent *stagnation*. Potpourris also feel stagnant after a while for the same reason. Fresh air is the best smell for bathrooms.

• Images of **animals** (including people) are also good. Animals symbolically have "the fire of life" and help to balance the Water element. However, avoid water animals—fish, dolphins, whales, crustaceans, or coral. Those images make a wet room wetter. You're in one big aquarium. Don't put shells in the bathroom, even as a soap dish.

• **Don't have pictures of water** or things associated with water (such as mermaids or surfboards) in the bathroom. Once again, that's too much wet vibe for an already wet room.

Bathroom in Wealth Corner

The far-left corner of the house is the Wealth Corner, sometimes called the Fortunate Blessings Area. It's perhaps the most important area of the feng shui bagua. (See Illustration 11.) If there's a bathroom in that corner, the drains symbolize money draining away. It signifies bad news financially or maybe bad news generally. I've steered many people away from pre-existing homes that have this problem, and I've talked many people out of putting Wealth Corner bathrooms in homes they were planning. Don't handicap your future by getting a home with a bathroom in the Wealth Corner.

A bathroom in the far-right corner is not a problem at all.

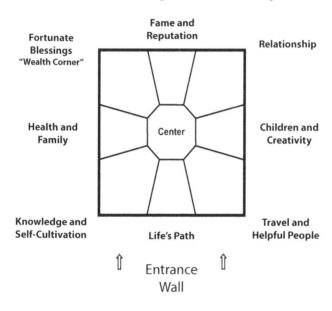

Illustration 11: The feng shui bagua

Remedies

Again, the only real cure is to remove the bathroom—put it anywhere else except, of course, the center. The symbolic remedies are the same as previously discussed, in the Central Bathroom section (*except* for the first two remedies of using the room less and adding adjacent mirrors).

It doesn't matter how often you use a Wealth Corner bathroom—what matters is how nice you keep it! The bathroom should be as deluxe as your pocketbook allows, and then some. You'll know you've done it right when you walk into your gorgeous bathroom and flinch at the memory of how much it cost to make the room so lovely.

Keep mirrors to a minimum in any Wealth Corner because they represent *windows* and, as such, opportunities for *wealth energy* to vanish out the window. One mirror over the sink is all any Wealth Corner bathroom should have.

Stairs in Line with Front Door

Don't buy a home with interior upward stairs in a direct line with the front door (see Illustration 12), unless you are willing to redirect the lower part of the stairs away from the door (see Illustration 13). Some of feng shui's greatest masters consider this to be the *most dire condition within a home*. The problem is most severe if the stairs are close to the door.

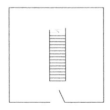 

**Illustration 12 (left): Stairs in line with front door
Illustration 13 (right): The lower stairs are moved.
The stairs no longer point to the front door.**

I should note this problem isn't an issue in a freestanding duplex. Often, one unit of a freestanding duplex is accessed by stairs going up as soon as the front door of the building is opened. If all the living space for that unit is upstairs (and that's usually the case), there is no problem.

Remedies

The only real remedy is to redirect the bottom few stairs as previously described. If you can't do this, don't buy the house. It's that serious. The real remedy is the only one that thoroughly keeps good energy from rolling right back out the door.

The following three remedies are symbolic and cannot truly surmount the problem but are still worth doing.

• A container (basket or umbrella stand) near the door will symbolically catch the energy. The container must not be completely full, and it can be empty.

• An inside mirror (preferably a bagua mirror), above or next to the door and on the same wall as the door, reflects the energy back into the house.

• A crystal (or a wind chime) hung between the stairs and the door disperses the energy that would otherwise leave too quickly.

Extremely Important Issues

These situations are almost as critical as the previous ones, but the remedies are either more thorough or more feasible.

Exterior

Landform

The best landform around a building is called the "armchair position." Visualize the building sitting in an armchair, facing out. The land in front slopes away from the building. The land behind the building slopes up, and there are smaller rises to each side of the house—like armrests. It's the ultimate symbol of protection. Homes with this landform configuration are so strong that any other feng shui problems are less serious. What you don't want is bad landform—especially if it's severe. If nothing backs up the home, it is symbolically sliding downhill. If the downhill slope behind the house is so steep that it's hard to walk, don't buy that home. Absolutely not! Shop across the street.

If the slope is slight, the problem is less. On flat land this is not an issue; the landscaping can symbolize good landform, with the tallest plantings behind the home.

A stream in front of the home brings good fortune, but behind a home the stream carries it away. If the stream is not on your property and not visible from your property, it is not a problem.

Remedies

• Put a weathervane somewhere noticeable on top of the building. This will counteract the slope behind the home. Things we notice early have a special strength. At the top of the house, the weathervane will be the highest thing, and it moves. We notice movement, so the energy is attracted upward. This lifts the entire energy of the home. If the weathervane shows an animal, *it should not be an underwater animal* like a whale or dolphin. For animal weathervanes, birds are best. If nice weathervanes are hard to find locally, I list an excellent Australian retailer in Sources (page 136).

• If a weathervane is out of the question, try to put something noticeable and preferably moving, such as a banner, above any part of the roof. It is not as powerful as a weathervane, but it's a step in the right direction.

• Add exterior lighting behind the home. It lifts and supports the back of the building. An example is a spotlight on a pole in the back yard facing the home. Although this is considered a strong remedy, it can look quite awkward behind some homes. Discreet uplights that highlight both plants and building are often preferred. The lights must shine *up* onto the building for this remedy to work.

Lights of any kind behind the building are better than no lights at all. Solar lights are quick and easy. Many small lights on a string or in a rope are a good solution when your options are limited. You could line the outside of a back window with them if nothing else would work. Don't use "icicle" lights because they symbolize energy dripping down.

• Put a fountain outside the front of the house. It can be on a porch. It needs to be running all the time, unless you're gone on vacation. If you're not going to keep the fountain going all the time, don't use this remedy. A fountain that isn't running but is on display says, "Dried up—broken!"

How the water flows is crucial in this instance. It must flow 360 degrees in all directions, like an umbrella.

Because some of the water flows away from the home, it counteracts the landform (which slopes upward away from the front of the house). Some of the water also flows directly toward the home. This symbolizes good fortune flowing into your life. Water represents money.

For any home, water flowing outside the front is good. In most instances, you want all the water flowing toward the home. Never, ever, have all the water flowing away from the home.

• Hang at least one mountain picture on the back wall of the home for *stability*. A picture is a window. What you see through the "window" is a mountain, so the mountain is symbolically placed behind the home. In this instance, don't use an image with an ocean or lake in the foreground. They represent an abyss. This remedy probably isn't as strong as the previous remedies, but it is often the only feasible remedy.

Size of Back Yard

Good fortune symbolically accumulates behind a house. If the back yard is too small, good fortune has a hard time accumulating. "Too small" is judged in relation to the front yard. The back yard should be as big or a bit bigger than the front yard. If the back yard is drastically smaller than the front, think twice about buying the house. That dynamic is going to be tough, and it may not be possible to fix completely.

Remedies

• Put a mirror at your back property line to symbolically expand the back yard. The mirror can be small, and it should face inward, toward your property. If the back yard is tiny and enclosed by a wood fence, consider putting a large mirror on the fence. It will really make the property seem larger.

• Paint a trompe l'oeil on the back yard fence. That is, create a scene with depth of perspective. This, too, will make the back yard seem larger.

Tree in Front of Front Door

A tree in a direct line between the front door and the street represents an obstacle. If the tree is off to the side, it's not a problem. It must be in an absolute direct line for it to be a problem. This doesn't apply to a front door opening toward woodland.

If you are willing to remove that particular tree as soon as you move in, it's okay to go ahead and buy the building.

There's an even rarer occurrence where a support post is directly in front of the front door. It's usually when the entrance is at a corner, and the door wall is at an angle. This does not refer to a post at the edge of a porch that you simply walk beside. I mean a post that you have to walk around to get to the door. You may use the remedies or take my best suggestion and skip that house.

Remedies

• If it doesn't look too strange above your front door, a bagua mirror is best in this situation. This is when I most strongly recommend these odd little mirrors for exteriors. Don't use a bagua mirror casually. It's not a good luck charm to put above a door to attract good fortune. Part of it is, after all, a mirror. Mirrors reflect and symbolically push away.

• If a bagua mirror won't work for you, any mirror, even a tiny mirror, will help the situation a lot. The mirror symbolically protects the building from the obstacle influence. It goes above the front door and reflects the obstacle away.

• You can change the purpose of the problem tree or pole from being an obstacle. You can make it a holder of affirmations by putting a written affirmation in the tree or on the pole. The affirmation can be as short as one word. Your creativity is really called into play for this remedy. If the tree has a low, wide crotch, you could place a stone there. You could use a stone with affirmative words carved into it or painted on it.

If the tree branches are high, don't use anything heavy. Perhaps use an affirmative coin akin to the ones recovery groups use. You can also etch your own affirmation by softly impressing words onto a piece of foil. A good example is, "Look up, be well." Press lightly with something like a dull pencil. Then hide the small piece of foil (or coin) in the tree (or on the post). It doesn't have to be seen to work. You put it there; it's working for you.

Risers on Front Stairs

If there are upward stairs leading to the front door, they need to have risers as well as treads. Treads are the part that your feet step on. The vertical piece that connects each tread to the next is the riser. It is what your toes point to as you walk up. If the stairs don't have risers, you see a gap between each tread. (See Illustration 14.) Chi energy slips through that gap. Stairs with risers conduct all the energy to your door. Stairs without them conduct only about ten percent of the energy. You would be missing a huge number of opportunities in such a home. The solution is to add risers, which is easy on wood stairs. If you are willing to do that soon after moving in, then go ahead and buy the house. If it isn't feasible to add risers, I strongly recommend not buying the house. If a condominium or apartment building has no risers on its stairs, but has an elevator, it's okay to live there.

Illustration 14: Side view of stairs with both treads and risers (left); side view of stairs with no risers (right)

Risers on interior stairs are important, but not nearly as important as those on exterior stairs to the front door.

Remedies

Add risers if possible. Anything else falls far short of a good remedy. Twining strands of tiny clear lights along the railing helps. You also must make your front door or the area just outside it very noticeable. Among the ways to do this:

- wind chimes
- wind catchers
- bright color
- a very gurgly fountain

It's okay to be a bit excessive in this instance; just don't overclutter the area.

Blue Roof

Don't buy a home or any building that has a blue roof, unless you're able to immediately change the roof to any other color. Blue is the only roof color that is unacceptable in feng shui. It portends money problems because it symbolizes water, which represents money. The money is seen to be flowing up over, and out of, your house—and your life.

Remedies

If other circumstances dictate that a blue-roofed house is the only one for you, here are two symbolic remedies that seem to help a lot.

- Hang or place a crystal above head height anywhere in the home. It symbolically disperses the roof's effect before it reaches your living space.

- Put any size mirror facing up, above head height, in the home. The mirror reflects and symbolically pushes away the effect of the roof.

A high ledge or attic is ideal for placing the crystal and/ or mirror. Both symbolic remedies can and should be used because they approach the problem from different angles. However, the best remedy for a blue roof is to change the roof color. (I had a client who painted over their blue roof and then later sold the home for a huge profit.)

Interior

Spiral Staircase

A staircase is considered spiral if it curves so tightly that some treads are directly above the treads below them. A spiral staircase is bad news anywhere inside a home because there's often some disorientation on arriving at a new level. Slight, perhaps, but feng shui pays great attention to that. The shape of the treads of spiral staircases is narrow and unsupportive. When the spiral staircase is fairly central in the home, the situation is considered quite horrible: "corkscrew through the heart." Don't get a home with this dynamic. I've seen homes like this, but never with great happiness among the occupants.

Remedies

The real remedy is to change the staircase so that it is no longer a spiral. Any other shape is fine for the stairs. If that's not possible:

- Hang a clear, faceted crystal above the staircase. Crystals symbolize dispersion because they can disperse the sun's energy into various rainbow colors. In this case, it symbolically disperses the spiral staircase energy in any location in a home. If a skylight is above the staircase, that's even better for getting maximum effect from a crystal. Any time a crystal actually receives sunlight, I prefer to use an octagon-shaped clear crystal. The prismatic colors are much more vivid and intense than with the disco ball–shaped crystal.

- Put an upward-shaped plant or plants near the bottom of the stairs to symbolically lift the energy. A good example of an upward-shaped plant is Sansevieria (snake plant or mother-in-law's tongue).

- I've heard of people using red ribbon or strands of artificial plants interwoven with the handrail supports to symbolically connect the two floors of the house. If you opt for this particular remedy, be sure not to create a safety hazard.

Excessive Windows

Johndennis Govert says in *Feng Shui: Art and Harmony of Place*: "People who live in glass houses shouldn't." Houses with entire walls of glass windows, especially **floor-to-ceiling windows**, and clear glass doors don't retain energy well. They don't fulfill the most basic feng shui requirement for a home—the sense of shelter is inadequate.

Skylights are a bright, welcoming feature in many homes, but they should never be directly above a bed, desk, or stove. Those three important areas should feel strong and protected. A skylight is a hole in an otherwise solid roof and the area directly under a skylight is therefore weakened.

Remedies

For excessive windows, install and use curtains, shades, screens, or blinds. They do an excellent job of retaining energy in a space. Natural fiber curtains are preferred because when artificial fibers photodegrade (break down) they release very tiny bits of plastic dust into your environment and the air you breathe. I often recommend silk because of how gracefully it moves in a breeze.

For a skylight in one of the three "wrong places" of bed, desk, or stove, hang a clear, faceted crystal from the center of the skylight. The crystal symbolically disperses the problematic energy of the skylight before it reaches the people below. I recommend the octagon shape for this use because it makes the best rainbow reflections.

To hang a crystal in the center of a skylight, affix strong, clear monofilament from side to side at the bottom of the skylight. At the center of that monofilament, hang a short piece of monofilament with the crystal attached.

Of Moderate Importance

Now that big problems have (hopefully) been ruled out, here are advantageous home attributes, as well as some things to watch out for. The feng shui implications for problems in these areas are average in intensity, and some of the situations are quite common, with many acceptable remedies.

Exterior

Moneybag Lot

A square or rectangle is generally considered the best lot shape, but there is one lot shape that is an improvement over a square or a rectangle. It is a trapezoid with the back larger than the front. (See Illustration 15.) This shape symbolizes a drawstring purse, where coins drop into the entrance, add up, and bulge out at the bottom. The back of the lot is the bottom of the moneybag. It holds good fortune well. Good fortune can come in many forms, including money.

Lots that are the *opposite shape*, with a larger entrance side and a smaller back side (see Illustration 16), are not auspicious. They are called dustpan lots and suggest good fortune will be pinched. Avoid buying property with that shape, but if there are overriding reasons to buy the property, there is one remedy.

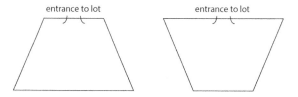

Illustration 15 (left): Moneybag lot shape
Illustration 16 (right): Dustpan lot shape

Remedies

The symbolic remedy for a *dustpan lot* is to put small mirrors outside on the property lines. On the right and left sides of your property, place mirrors aimed in toward your property. If you don't have a wall or fence to put them on, you can use stakes. They should be located toward the back of your lot, not toward the front. Their purpose is to *expand* your property, and that's what you should say out loud when you install them.

Front Door

The front door should be immediately noticeable when you arrive at the house. It is the mouth of the home. A very noticeable front door ensures that energy will find you. The reason some people paint front doors red in feng shui is to make them obvious. If the door is already noticeable, there is little or no need for that.

A hidden front door suggests that energy will have a hard time finding you. I once arrived at a client's home and spent the next fifteen minutes trying to find the front door. When I did, no one was home. She had written the wrong time on her calendar. Energy was missing her.

A main entrance on the side of the house is bad enough, but on the back of a house it is horrible. If someone has to pass by one or more auxiliary doors on the way to the main door, it invites confusion into your life.

Remedies

To avoid greeting chi energy with a question mark, make it extremely obvious how to get to the front door. A spacious paved pathway to the door is essential. Stepping-stones are not enough.

• Use signage to draw attention to the pathway—"The Joneses" or "Welcome."

• Attract attention with motion, sound, and/or bright color close by the door. Suggestions include wind chimes, wind catchers, or a fountain.

Exterior Poison Arrows

"Poison arrow" might sound hokey. It has other names—sha chi or shar chi in Chinese. It's really just harsh energy that a body can (usually subconsciously) feel from a nearby foreboding object. Imagine a sharp pencil held very close to your eye. Some people would develop a twitch even though nothing actually touched their eye. That's how poison arrows work. Divide a sharp right angle in half to see where one aims.

See Illustrations 17 and 18 for examples of poison arrows coming from neighboring buildings.

Illustration 17 (left): Poison arrow created by neighboring building
Illustration 18 (right): Poison arrow from another house

Remedies

• Build a solid fence or plant an evergreen hedge so you can't see the neighboring corner from your house. If you don't see that poison arrow, it's not there—as far as feng shui is concerned.

- If a fence or hedge is unfeasible, use a mirror to symbolically reflect the harsh energy away from your house. Use a small flat mirror or a convex mirror. Since it's outside your home, you can also use a bagua mirror.

Interior

Regularly Shaped Building

House styles change over time, but the basic feng shui rules stay the same. **Square houses** (like many Craftsman or Mission-style homes) or **rectangular houses** (like many Mid-century Ranch houses) are considered to have the best shapes. Much importance is placed on the **form** or **shape** of the building. Having four external corners is ideal. Five or more external corners on a home starts to be problematic. Earlier, I discussed the importance of having the two back corners in place. Those are just the two most important corners. All four corners and all the areas of a perfect square (or perfect rectangle) are important. When a building is "more interesting" than a square or rectangle, it suggests that some area of a person's life might be handicapped. See the section on the bagua to learn more (page 99).

Not all missing areas are in corners. Sometimes missing areas can happen along the side of a wall. Illustration 19 shows a missing area in the middle of the back wall.

**Illustration 19:
The Fame area is missing in the middle of the back wall.**

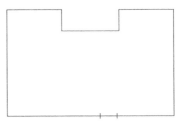

Remedies

• If possible, put something significant at the exact spot where the corner would be. (That would be Point A in Illustrations 20 and 21.)

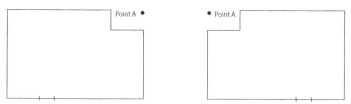

Illustrations 20 & 21: Remedying a missing corner by placing something significant where the corner should be

• If the building is missing any of the four corners, put a mirror or mirrors on one or both of the walls tangent to the missing area. The reflective side should face into the room. The mirror symbolically enlarges the building. (See Illustrations 22 and 23.)

Illustrations 22 & 23: Remedying a missing corner by using mirrors

• If the missing area occurs in the middle of a wall (not in a corner) put mirrors as shown in Illustration 24. Remember to put the reflective side toward the room.

Illustration 24: Using mirrors to remedy a missing area in the middle of a wall

Two other examples of irregularly shaped homes are split levels and L-shaped homes.

The caution concerning **split-level houses** is that they can symbolize splitting up or breaking apart. Split-levels can feel awkward when they don't seem to work naturally with the landform of the lot. Often the split-level design is used as a novelty with no reference to the slope of the land.

Remedies

• If there is a landing directly inside the front door, hang a crystal up high in the center of the landing. A chandelier is fine if that works with your style.

• Draw the eye toward the living room. Then you are not presenting chi with the question, "Which way is the living room?"

An **L-shaped house** is called a meat cleaver shape. One wall is the "blade" wall and is not auspicious. To find the blade wall, locate the *longest* wall, then look for the parallel wall on the other side of the house that is *farthest from* the longest wall. (See Illustration 25.) It is considered dangerous, especially to health. Don't spend a lot of time at that wall. It's not a good place for this furniture:

• the head of a bed

• a favorite lounge chair or couch

• your desk

• your usual dining seat

Remedies

If one of these pieces of furniture must be against the blade wall, put a mirror on the opposite side of the room, facing into the room. The mirror symbolically moves the furniture (and person) to the inner wall. (See Illustration 26.) Usually, mirrors at the foot of the bed are not recommended in feng shui. This is an exception.

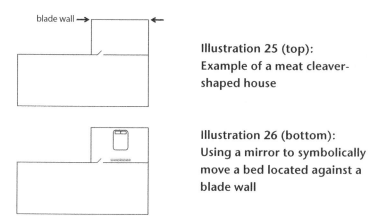

Illustration 25 (top): Example of a meat cleaver-shaped house

Illustration 26 (bottom): Using a mirror to symbolically move a bed located against a blade wall

L-Shaped Rooms

L-shaped rooms are considered incomplete. A mirror completes them.

Remedy

Illustration 27 shows where to put the mirror. You have a choice of two walls. Feel free to mirror both walls—the bigger, the better. Don't use mirror tiles, though, because they break up your image.

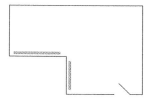

Illustration 27: L-shaped room with mirrors to remedy the incomplete room

Interior Poison Arrows

Poison arrows can originate within a house. A right angle that protrudes into a room aims a poison arrow across the room. (See Illustration 28.) On a carpeted floor, you can trace the path of the poison arrow with your finger and see exactly where it goes. Divide the right angle in half and follow it across the room. Don't sleep or regularly sit in the path of a poison arrow. A part of your body would always be subtly "on guard" because something is pointing directly at you.

**Illustration 28:
A room with a sharp
right-angle indent
creating a poison arrow**

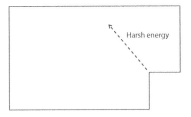

Remedies

• Bullnose the corner. Say those words to any builder; they'll know what to do. They will slightly round the tip of the corner so that energy will flow around the corner instead of aiming out. (See Illustration 29.) The vibration of the house will be forever strengthened. This is a real remedy. The problem is absolutely gone.

**Illustration 29: The
sharp corner from
Illustration 28 has been
bullnosed (rounded).**

• Block the path of the arrow with a tall object—
plant, screen, or shelving. This can be an awkward
constraining factor when decorating. The previous
remedy will free up your furniture arranging.

Defined Rooms

Rooms are areas within the house that are physically
defined by walls or other architectural features. Separate
rooms for separate purposes are preferred in feng shui. The
two most common places where this problem occurs are with
ensuite bathrooms and great rooms. **Ensuite bathrooms**
are sadly becoming more popular, but great rooms are
thankfully becoming passé.

I've mentioned before that bathrooms are problematic.
Their energy is wet, heavy, drain-down, body waste —
altogether *too yin* to be influencing the rest of the house.
You especially don't want it influencing the place where you
sleep. Don't buy a house with an ensuite bathroom unless
you are willing to install a door between the bedroom and
the bathroom.

Remedy

Curtains will do until you get the door installed. They
are not a permanent solution. The door to the bathroom *has*
to be closed when you are sleeping. If need be, it can be left
ajar during the day for air circulation.

Great rooms were a regrettable post-mid-century
phenomenon. People are better off with more *defined* rooms.
I've been to hundreds of homes with great rooms, and I've
been to an equal number of homes with separate rooms for
different purposes. Craftsman-style homes (sometimes called
Mission-style) are frequently good feng shui choices for homes.

They have defined rooms and they usually have both back corners, since many of the Craftsman homes were square.

Remedy

If you will be living with a great room, I recommend using tall furniture, screens, or tall plants to define use areas. You will appreciate the results in your life.

Open Beams

A flat ceiling without open beams is ideal. A slanted ceiling or open beams cause a part of the room to have more pressurized energy. The effect is more pressure in your life, and possibly health problems. The beams (and this applies to fake beams, too) hold up the pressure of the roof. That feeling of pressure continues directly below the beam. The lowest part of a slanted ceiling also applies pressure to the space below it. A slanted ceiling that is quite high is not a problem. The higher the beams, the less negative their effect on people. Very high beams, painted the ceiling color, are not a problem at all.

Remedies

This is a fairly common problem and there are many remedies to choose from.

- If the beams are fake (non-structural), remove them.

- Add a ceiling below the beams that hides them. In feng shui, to hide something is to erase it.

- Tack fabric below the beams to create a fabric ceiling. This is sometimes done above a bed.

- Paint the beams to match the ceiling so they are less noticeable.

• Hang a crystal or wind chimes from a beam that is directly over a bed or seating. They symbolize dispersing the heavy energy before it reaches the living bodies below.

• If possible, avoid locating beds or seating directly under the beams or the lowest part of a ceiling. Especially try to avoid putting the head of a bed under the lowest part of a slanted ceiling.

• Bamboo flutes are a standard feng shui remedy, but they can look out of place in some homes. Hang a flute from each end of the beam at a tilt so the mouthpiece is angled down. This position symbolizes playing the flute, because the mouthpiece is aimed a bit downward for ease of use. When blowing a flute in this direction, your breath (the wind) is going upward; thus, the symbolism of lifting the heavy beam. The two flutes should hang close to the two side walls.

Nice to Have, Easy to Fix

The situations covered here are primarily desirable features that harmonize and empower a building. If there is a problem in any of these areas, the remedies are strong, easy, and varied.

Exterior

Away from Highways

The home's proximity to the road and exposure to traffic sounds determines how restful the home will feel. A house right next to a very busy road suffers from having its energy chipped away. Each vehicle wears away at the peace of the home. Deep rest is more elusive.

Remedies

• Plant an evergreen hedge or build a solid fence across the front of the lot to block the harsh energy. This is the best remedy because the disturbance is blocked at the boundary of the property, before reaching the house. Then the yard can be a peaceful buffer zone surrounding the home. The extra peace is real, not symbolic. This remedy is good on its own, but even better combined with the next remedy.

• Put a small mirror outside the home facing the road. A convex mirror is best, and a bagua mirror is even better. This remedy is a powerful addition to the previous remedy. If you have a high hedge or wall and can't see the road from your house, put the mirror on the *outside* of the wall or hedge. The mirror works best when it actually reflects back the traffic images. A multistory dwelling with a solid fence would still need a mirror on each upper level. If you can see the traffic from your home, you need a mirror.

T-Intersection

Harsh energy is projected at a building at the exact end of a T-intersection. (See Illustration 30.) While it's ideal if your home isn't at the end of the intersection, it's an easily solved problem.

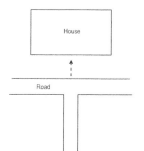

**Illustration 30:
The location of this home at the end of a T-intersection is not favorable.**

Remedies

• The remedies in the previous section should be repeated here, in addition to the remedy below.

• Use reflectors along the road boundary of your property. Some are ready-made with a ground pin. Use whatever color you prefer, but keep it to one color.

Curved Roads

A convex curve is the beginning of an angle pointing at you. It's not horribly bad if you're on the convex side, but being on the concave side is always much better. Houses on the concave side of a curved road are more protected than those on the convex side. (See Illustration 31.) Think of a sharp, curved knife, like a machete or scimitar. The convex side is sharp and dangerous. When cars move along the road, their headlights shine on the houses on the convex side, not the concave side. Their lights are an uninvited intrusion. Homes at the very end of a cul-de-sac have this problem.

Illustration 31: The best side of a curved road is the concave side.

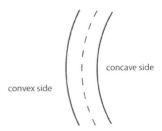

convex side

concave side

Remedies

Houses on the convex side should have an evergreen hedge or solid fence in front to protect them. If that isn't immediately possible, put a small convex mirror outside the front of the house. Try to place it at the height at which car lights strike the house. Because it bulges outward, the mirror reflects energy from many directions. Such mirrors are inexpensive and available where auto supplies are sold.

Neighboring Buildings

There are several things that are considered troublesome if they are *directly next to* a residence—cemeteries, mortuaries, police stations, fire stations, and churches. Cemeteries and mortuaries are a problem because of the possibility of wandering spirits. Police and fire stations are, of course, noisy because of sirens. They can also impart a vibration of chaos to their near neighbors. This is because the people who work there must frequently respond to chaos.

Feng shui is a friend to all religions, but it does not recommend living next door to a church. There are three reasons for this. Funerals happen there, so there is the possibility of wandering, confused spirits. Many churches sit vacant and unused for long periods of time, and therefore take on an excessive yin vibration. This is not appropriate next to a residence, which should be more yang (active). Also, the physical shape of a sharp steeple is seen to be similar to a drawn sword, and therefore unfriendly.

Schools are not a problem from a feng shui point of view. Elementary schools are seen as auspicious because of the young, yang, active vibration.

Remedies

The best remedy is a bagua mirror placed outside the home and facing the problematic area. If the mirror cannot be placed outside your home (because of home association restrictions, etc.), put it in a window directly against the windowpane and faced away from your home. If a bagua mirror is not acceptable, use any mirror. Windows and doors are places where a building is most vulnerable. When they face a problematic area, they should have a mirror (preferably bagua) above them outside.

If your home is next to a cemetery or mortuary, keep a low-wattage light on every night in front of a sacred image. If you use a Buddha image, the full lotus posture (meditating with legs crossed) is the most protective position. The image can be anywhere in the home, preferably at or above the level of your heart.

Entering Through the Front Door

The front door is the grandest door and it's best if the residents come and go through that door when leaving and arriving back home. If a less attractive door is used on a regular basis—such as a garage or carport door—that's less ideal. It's not horrible, but it's definitely *less ideal*.

Remedy

This problem is definitely not a deal breaker, because your own behavior can fix the problem. Just arrive home through your official front door at least once a month. Park your car (if you have one) and then come around to your front door, unlock it, and enter the home that way—the grand way. I've gone to homes where the front-door hinges were rusty, and the door had cobwebs—fresh energy is not being welcomed into the home. Since my client never entered the home through her front door, she was unaware of the situation.

Pool Location

The worst location for an in-ground pool is directly behind the house. It symbolizes an abyss and fails to give the home proper backing and support. Any other location is preferable.

If a pool is curved, the concave part should be closest to the house. The area inside a curve is more protected than the outside (convex) part.

Infinity edge pools are never recommended because the flow of the water is always away from the home. Water represents money and good fortune and should always flow toward the home, not away from it. There's no good way to symbolically fix this problem—you'd need to put a cement lip all the way around the top edge of the pool.

Shallow decorative ponds are okay anywhere, as are above-ground pools.

Remedies

• Put a small mirror outside the house facing the problem pool. The mirror pushes away the influence of the pool.

• Put plants, even potted plants, between the house and pool—the taller, the better. They uplift the area and create a separation.

Interior

Bedroom Door Location

Your bed is the most important object in the home. You spend a third of your life there. Good bed placement is key to a successful life. Here are some of the most important rules.

The number-one rule is to be able to easily see the door from the bed. The door represents the future. When lying in bed with your head propped on a pillow, you should be able to see the main door into the room. (See Illustration 32.) If you have to crane your neck to see that door, you are setting up a dynamic in your life that things will surprise you. Events will seem to "come out of left field" and you won't be prepared for them.

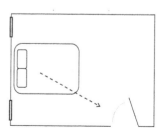

Illustration 32: An empowered bed position. You can easily see the doorway.

Remedy

If it isn't feasible to place the bed in the correct position, use a mirror to see the door. (See Illustration 33.) Put the mirror at the right height and angle so that if you are lying in bed, the reflection of the doorway is plainly visible in the mirror. A freestanding dressing mirror can do the job well and not look out of place. You might consider using a convex mirror or a large gazing ball instead of a flat mirror. The problem with a convex mirror is that it shouldn't be used as a mirror to see yourself. You should not use it to check your hair or see how your clothes look. If you use a convex mirror, try to arrange things so that you won't be tempted to use it for that purpose. Seeing oneself in a mirror is akin to knowing oneself. If your reflection is distorted, it will be more difficult for you to have a true awareness of who you really are. A gazing ball is an excellent alternative that fits well into many decors. They are silvered reflective balls that are intended for use in a garden. Nicely mounted, they look good indoors.

Illustration 33: A mirror placed as indicated allows you to see the door from the bed.

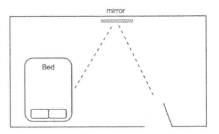

Some feng shui consultants suggest angling the head of the bed in the corner of the room. I don't recommend angling a bed except as a last resort. Beds are more protected and restful when the headboard is parallel and close to a solid wall. An angled bed can create an unused, stagnant space behind the headboard. If there is no choice but to angle the bed, put a tall houseplant in the vacant space between the headboard and the corner. What used to be a stagnant space is now creating oxygen.

Harsh Energy from Doorway

Chi energy enters a room through the entrance door. A swath of strong chi energy the width of the door passes directly across the room from front wall to back wall. (See Illustration 34.) *Make sure the bed is not located in that swath of energy.* It is too harsh, and the bed should be located elsewhere in the room. (See Illustration 35.)

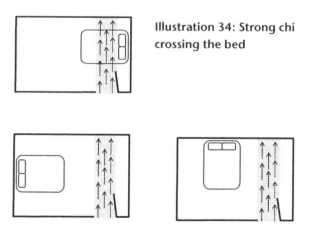

Illustration 34: Strong chi crossing the bed

Illustration 35: Good bed positions

It is particularly important that you do not place the bed fully in the swath of chi energy with your feet facing the door. That's called the "coffin position" because coffins are carried through doorways feet first.

Remedies

If there is no choice but to have a bed located in that swath of energy, some sort of buffer or screen should be placed between the door and the bed. Examples are:

- an armoire or large chest

- a folding screen

- tall plants with thick foliage (good artificial ones will do fine)

- a curtain—even sheers will work

- a beaded curtain, if that works with the decor

- a very thick, patterned rug

- a crystal or wind chime hung between the door and the bed (symbolizing breaking up and slowing down harsh, fast energy)

Distance Between Toilet and Bed

There is a problem if the head of the bed is against a wall that has a bathroom drain on the other side. The drain energy is too close to the person's head. The worst situation is a toilet that flushes directly behind the head of the bed.

Remedies

- Put a small mirror on the wall behind the toilet tank, facing the toilet. If a sink is behind the head of a bed, affix the mirror to the wall, under the counter, reflective side toward the sink basin. This creates a better separation between the bed and the drain.

- Put a heavy weight under the sink or by the toilet next to the wall. It represents grounding so the drains cannot affect your good fortune.

Central Staircase

A staircase in the center of a home is not going to ruin your life. It can, however, bring more chaos and craziness. Chi energy can run in circles around such areas (known as whirlwind or racetrack), as do young children and pets.

Remedies

• Place a soft rug on the floor somewhere around the stairs. You can do this even if the area is carpeted. It slows the energy because your feet are on a softer surface and they're tempted to linger.

• Hang a crystal, wind chime, or mobile from the ceiling above or near the stairs. It will help disperse fast energy.

Features Representing Disharmony

There are certain features that represent disagreement. These three are the most problematic.

Kitchen Appliances

Most important is the location of appliances representing the feng shui Elements (see Glossary, page 134) of Fire and Water in the kitchen. The sink and refrigerator are Water. The stove is Fire. Fire and Water are opposites in feng shui. Conflict is common if they are exactly next to each other or directly across from each other. When they are across from each other and there is an island between them, a problem is unlikely.

Remedy

If the stove (oven or rangetop) is directly across from the refrigerator or sink, hang a crystal from the ceiling between the two appliances to symbolize dispersion.

It's practical to have counter space on each side of the stove top, but occasionally, even in large kitchens, the refrigerator is right next to the stove top. I've seen scorch marks on the side of the refrigerator from stoves placed too closely. It's poor design and seriously bad feng shui. Moving the appliances is rarely feasible, so use a crystal to symbolically fix the situation. Put the crystal directly above the small gap between the two appliances to disperse their conflicting energies. The crystal can also be put in a cabinet above the refrigerator or stove, as close to the gap as possible. If the refrigerator is built in and surrounded by wood cabinetry, the problem is less severe.

Central Support Pole

A support pole in the middle of a room represents disagreement. One eye sees one side, and the other eye sees the other side. "I see things one way." "I see things a different way." If you live alone, it can suggest uncertainty in your own mind.

Remedy

Put a tall object next to the pole. Use tall furniture, a tall plant, or a screen. Even a hanging plant that twines around the pole will work. The pole blends with other objects and is less important. A pole at the edge of a space (such as a porch) is not a problem.

Clashing Doorknobs

If the knobs or handles of two different doors can touch each other, they are called "clashing knobs." They represent two heads knocking against each other. This does not apply to kitchen cabinets.

Remedy

Rehang one of the doors so the knobs can't touch. If that's not possible, hang a red ribbon or red tassel from each knob that can touch another knob. The red represents blood and says, "There's *new blood*—a new dynamic is happening."

Quality Building Materials

Blessed is the person whose home is made of quality materials. And sad is the person whose home was built using shoddy materials. If the building is inspected by a professional before the purchase, then there's probably nothing to be concerned about. I've watched building inspectors go about their work—they are thorough. The feng shui concern with shoddy building materials is very basic— the protection that your home appears to offer must be real.

Remedy

Don't buy a home without having it professionally inspected. Don't get into a situation where you have to replace low-quality building materials—unless you know about it in advance and your offering price reflects that knowledge. In Recommended Reading (page 72) I suggest books on home inspection.

Other Considerations

These are a few situations that don't occur in most homes, but they do occur often enough to merit discussion because of the severity of the problems they portend.

Exterior

Driveway Slope

Where the driveway meets the road, it should be fairly level so energy rolls in evenly. If the driveway slopes down steeply as it goes toward the house, you shouldn't buy the property. (See Good Landform, page 20.) If the driveway slopes steeply uphill as it goes toward the house, energy coming to the house is likely to roll back down to the road before reaching the house.

Remedy

If the driveway slopes steeply uphill from the road, put a small mirror in a discreet location. It should be at the beginning of the driveway, reflecting up the driveway. It will reflect back energy that would otherwise roll out to the road.

Smaller of Opposite Driveways

When two driveways are directly opposite each other, they are in competition for luring chi energy. The larger one wins.

Remedy

If you cannot increase the size of your driveway, make

it more noticeable. Use plants or ornamentation to make your driveway entrance stunning. Heads should turn toward your driveway. Use bright or noticeable sculpture, pottery, or plants (but not spiky-leaf plants). Lovely pavement on the driveway surface could remedy this situation very well. Even an arresting mailbox would work.

Semicircular Front Steps

The front steps of a building, leading to the front door, should not be shaped like a semicircle. That shape symbolizes wealth pouring away from the building. You want wealth to be pouring into the building. The best stairs are regular non-curved stairs, and luckily that's the shape of most stairs.

The reason that semicircular stairs have that problematic symbolism is because the lip of a pitcher for pouring water has a curved shape where the water leaves the pitcher, and (in feng shui) water symbolizes money and good fortune.

Remedy

Be prepared to change the shape of the stairs so they are not semicircular. Otherwise, don't buy the home.

Fake Shutters and Mullions

Both these problems are important, but thankfully they're not terribly common (anymore) and each has a real solution. I don't recommend symbolic solutions for these problems. Things that are noticeable outside of your home (especially in the front of your home) have a very strong influence on the energy of the home. They are noticed first, and *things that are noticed first are most important.*

These problems have to do with the windows, and windows represent the eyes—how we view things. We need the support of true, accurate discernment in our decision making—and fake things in or near the windows symbolize trusting in facts that are untrue.

Fake shutters don't cover the windows when they are closed. They aren't intended to move. They look fake and they scream fake from a feng shui point of view. You may think that the house needs the shutters to look good, but the vertical shape of shutters does not serve to ground the residents. Fake shutters also say "lack of protection" because the protection they seem to offer isn't real.

Real, functioning shutters are very good feng shui because the protection they offer is real, not just symbolic.

Remedy

The problem is not a minor one, but the remedy is quite simple—remove the shutters. The house will look better.

Mullions are strips that divide the separate glass panes in traditional windows. (They're sometimes called muntins or window grilles.)

Fake mullions are never necessary. They have the same energetic problem as fake shutters—a susceptibility to delusion. The difference between the two types of mullions is very plain to see—real mullions are a structurally integrated part of the window, whereas fake ones are either suspended between double-paned glass or adhered to the glass surface.

Remedy

The remedy is simple but not always easy or cheap. Replace the windows that have fake mullions with windows that have no mullions. If the fake mullions (usually plastic) are the stick-on type, the solution will fortunately be both free and easy—just permanently remove them. You will enjoy the views from your windows much more.

Interior

Foyers

The foyer is the *ming tang* or "bright hall." It is where chi energy receives its first impression of your home. What one notices when arriving in the foyer is important. For one thing, the location of the living room needs to be fairly obvious. It is also important to retain chi energy in the home before it vanishes too quickly.

When a window or back door is directly opposite and visible from the front door, energy zooms out. A good view is wonderful, but it must not be the feature first noticed upon entering. That sort of home does not adequately contain energy. If possible, shop for houses on the other side of the road. They probably have the same great view, just not on the back side of the house.

Remedies

Place a screen between the front door and the back door or windows. This is an excellent real remedy and is preferred in feng shui.

Hanging sheer curtains over the back windows is also a wonderful real remedy. Light can pour into the room, but chi energy also stays in. Don't rule sheer curtains out as a remedy until you've done some shopping.

The next two remedies are symbolic and will do if the previous remedies aren't feasible. They are also nice adjuncts to the sheer curtain remedy.

• Hang a crystal or wind chime between the front door and the back door or window to disperse the energy into the home.

• Put a mirror on the back wall next to the back door or window to reflect the energy back into the home.

Room Location and Proportion

Yin and Yang Rooms

Rooms with an active purpose (living room or office) are best in the front part of the house. They benefit from the busy yang energy of the road. Rooms with a quiet purpose (bedrooms) benefit from the restful yin energy toward the back of the house. It's also good not to have bedrooms directly above or behind a garage. The busy influence of the car is inappropriately close.

Remedies

• If bedrooms are close to a road or other busy influence, place a mirror (preferably outside) facing the disturbance. The mirror can be very small, less than an inch in diameter. It is ideal to use a convex mirror if the disturbance is a road. The bulge of the mirror pushes back the cars in many directions.

• Use plenty of fabric, such as heavy curtains, and a layered window treatment in any room that needs to be more restful. Use quiet colors.

• If active rooms are in the rear of the house, use lighter, more open furniture and at least a touch of bright color. Use less fabric.

• If the cars in a garage point directly at a wall that is tangent to a bedroom, put a small mirror in the garage. The mirror should be at headlight level, with the reflective side facing the car. The mirror reflects and symbolically pushes the car away.

• If the bedroom is over a garage, put a mirror (any size) on the ceiling of the garage, with the reflective side facing the car. Place the mirror either directly over the automobile or directly under the bed. Occasionally the ceiling of the garage is not a good option for the mirror. In that case, put the mirror in the bedroom under the bed, reflective side down.

• You can also hang a crystal on the ceiling of the garage above the car or cars. The crystal disperses the busy energy of the car before it reaches the quiet bedroom.

Ceiling Height

It's usually obvious when a ceiling is too low. The space feels cramped. Ceilings can also be too high and not contain energy well. It's difficult to feel settled in such homes. Very high ceilings are more suited for businesses than homes.

Remedies for low ceilings

• Paint them white so they feel more expansive.

• Use uplights—lights that shine upward. They lift the oppressive energy.

Remedies for high ceilings

• Paint them a bit darker than usual to make them seem lower.

• Install crown molding around the walls some distance below the ceiling. Paint the wall above the molding the same color as the ceiling.

• Most of the light should be directed downward. Pools of light on the floor will make it cozier.

• The furniture should be dark, substantial, and heavy-looking to ground energy.

Long Halls

Long halls speed energy along too quickly. The wider the better for long halls. A long, narrow hall is similar to a rifle barrel—the energy just shoots right through.

Remedies

• Hang artwork on the wall and/or from the ceiling. Make it an art gallery—preferably a tactile gallery where the art invites touch. Wall sculptures and wall hangings are good, as well as pictures without glass covering. You could hang a mobile from the ceiling.

• Hang a crystal from the ceiling. Its purpose is to symbolically disperse the energy that is going too fast.

• Make sure the lighting invites you to linger.

• Side doors along the hall should be left open or ajar to distract and slow the energy. However, if the door is to a bathroom or closet, leave it closed.

• Add a rug or rugs on the floor. It should have an interesting pattern, but not stripes, which portend arguments. (I have a video discussion on this topic posted on my website.)

Toilet and Stove Proximity

There shouldn't be a toilet exactly behind the stove, sharing the same wall. The stove symbolizes money, so this situation suggests that those opportunities are flushed away before reaching you.

Remedies

• Put a small mirror on the wall behind the toilet tank, facing the toilet. It symbolically keeps the vibrations of the toilet from going through the wall.

• Put one or two big, rounded stones on the floor beside the toilet, but out of the way. They symbolize stillness. They are mountains, and nothing moves mountains. Flushes come and go, but that activity is nulled by the still, large stones.

Fireplace/Stove Location

A fireplace or stove should not be in the center of a room. They should be within six feet of a wall. Also, an open fireplace in a direct line with the front door offers chi the opportunity to go up and out the chimney immediately.

Remedy

• The real remedy is to move the fireplace or the stove.

• Put an opaque screen, large picture, or plant arrangement in front of the firebox (the cavity where wood is burned). Keep it there any time a fire is not lit.

Rarities

Although the following seven situations are rare, they are *very problematic.*

Exterior

A-Frame

The shape of an A-frame building is too severe to be conducive to a balanced life. The problem is less severe if all the downstairs rooms have vertical walls. Spending a good bit of time in a room with walls that slope inward at the top is not good for a person, and symbolic remedies can't change that.

My only advice: Avoid buying this shape of house.

Roof with No Overhang

This symbolizes inadequate protection for a *freestanding* home. There is no ill consequence for apartment and condo buildings without an overhanging roof.

Remedy

Make a roof with an overhang. That's really the only solution. The cheapest would probably be a faux mansard roof with an overhang.

Barren Yard

The best yards have lush, healthy landscaping. If there is grass, but not much else, start planting. Plants with rounded leaves are preferred. Avoid thorny or very spiky-leaved plants. Their energy is threatening and unfriendly.

The worst yards are totally paved. A paved yard stifles the energy from the earth and makes a place look barren.

Remedies

The best solution for a totally paved yard is to remove some of the concrete. If that cannot be done, stain it an earth tone and add some flower boxes or potted plants.

Interior

Bathroom and Kitchen Proximity

A kitchen should not have a door that opens directly into a bathroom. This situation suggests health problems because the rooms have opposite functions and are too close.

Remedies

• Keep the bathroom door closed. This must be done. Use a self-closing hinge if necessary. They're easy to install. The best thing that can be done for any bathroom is to keep the door closed.

• Put a mirror on the outside of the bathroom door to reflect chi away from the room.

• Put a mirror above or beside the bathroom door, on the wall outside the bathroom. This reflects chi away when the bathroom door is opened.

Entrance Door in Line with Exit Door

In decorating terminology, enfilade doors are aligned along a single axis—the entrance door is in an exact line with an exit door to a room. (You could walk into the room and without changing direction at all, walk out an exit door.) Three such doors in an *exact* line (Illustration 36) are a *major* feng shui problem, especially when all three doors are interior doors. They confuse chi energy in a unique way causing it not to disperse into the rooms properly.

Illustration 36 (top):
Three doors in a row
(enfilade doors)

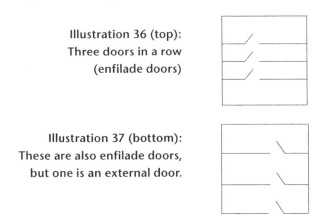

Illustration 37 (bottom):
These are also enfilade doors,
but one is an external door.

The problem is less of a concern if one of the doors is external. Not two of the doors, *one* of the doors, as in Illustration 37. If two of the three doors are external, don't consider buying the home. Energy won't ever stay in the home properly unless one of the doors is moved.

This is not the same as three doors side-by-side (Illustration 38) which is usually quite harmonious.

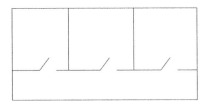

Illustration 38: Three doors side by side. Not a problem.

Remedies

The only real remedy is to move one of the doors, as in Illustration 39. My advice is to do this or don't buy the house.

Illustration 39: One of the enfilade doors has been moved. They are no longer in a direct line.

The standard symbolic remedy is to hang one or more crystals anywhere above the pathway through the doors of each room. Although this is a practical remedy in most situations, I doubt that it ever completely overcomes this particular problem when there are three or more doors in a line.

Two Mirrors Facing Each Other

Two mirrors that face each other are a major feng shui problem, and other disciplines also look askance at this situation. I consulted for a couple who told me that in shamanism, facing mirrors are considered to open a portal to malevolent, non-human energies. I believe it because of the stories that my clients (who have had facing mirrors) have told me—very ghostly, very malevolent.

Remedies

Even though this is a bad problem, it's super easy to fix. Either cover or remove one of the two mirrors that face each other. If they are sliding closet doors, they are easy to remove: raise them slightly, remove them from their lower track, flip them around backward, and reinsert them into the lower track. If two facing mirrors are in a bathroom, consider covering one of them with frosted contact paper or contact paper with a stained-glass pattern.

Glass (Clear) Floors and Stairs

Want a problem? You can even pay extra for it! Clear walking surfaces are seen (by some) as glamorous, but what they really are is stupid because they go against the wisdom of trusting your own eyesight. **Glass floors are a feng shui nightmare**, and even if it's just a part of a floor surface, it's still an awful problem. The nightmare becomes even worse when stairs are made of clear glass—energy completely misses the transition from floor to floor. And can you imagine falling on glass stairs? Clear walking surfaces are the ultimate proof of the adage "Just because you *can* do something, doesn't mean you *should*." Just because thick glass or acrylic floors are possible doesn't mean you should fall for the fad.

Special Situations

Raw Land

Lot Shape

Don't buy property that has a triangular outline. It's not good to live on, and it can be a problem to sell. The best lot shapes are square or rectangular. They excel because of their regularity. Nothing is "missing," and no corners are pinched. The only shape better is a moneybag lot, a trapezoid with the back side longer than the entrance side. (See Illustration 40.) Money and good fortune symbolically collect in the back, just as a drawstring purse gets bigger at the bottom when coins are added.

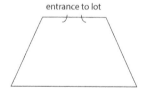
entrance to lot

**Illustration 40:
An auspicious moneybag-shaped lot**

Landform for House

If you are buying land on which to build your house, look for good landform. The land should rise up behind the house site, but not too steeply. Ideally, there should also be a slight rise on each side of the house site. The land in front of the house site should slope down and away from the house. If there is a natural water feature, it should be in front of the house site, not behind it. A house built in this "armchair position" is powerful because the land protects it without obstructing.

Commercial Properties

Business property is more yang than residential property because it's about activity; money is earned there. The foremost feng shui concern for businesses is to attract chi energy. People need to find your business, and their money certainly won't find you if they can't. Make it easy for customers or clients to find you. Get an obvious, well-trafficked location. A corner location is ideal for a business because a corner is seen from two roads, not just one.

There is usually no problem if a commercial property lot has an odd shape—even a triangular lot shape is not a disadvantage for business property. Once again, it's the yang nature of business that overcomes what would be a disadvantage in residential property, with a freestanding house. Triangular lot shapes can even be used to great advantage in these circumstances—think of New York City's Flatiron Building.

Offices

If the property slopes, the main entrance to the offices should be on the downhill side of the building. That gives you good landform because the building has symbolic backing from the land around it. In a very urban environment, the main concern is that no next-door buildings dwarf yours. They can be bigger, just not a lot bigger—you don't want your property to look insignificant. The larger building depletes the chi energy that should be entering your building. The remedy is to put a mirror outside your building with the reflective side pointed at the very tall building. Any mirror will help, but a *concave* bagua mirror is best in this instance. The concave mirror will flip the image upside-down, thereby reducing its importance. If there are poison arrows pointing at your building, use mirrors to deflect them. (See page 31 for Illustrations 17 and 18 of poison arrows.)

Retail

Location, location, location. They're the first three common-sense rules about retail. People need to easily see your store, or at least your signage. If they can't find you, you won't prosper.

A good landform would be a nice plus, as would no poison arrows, but they are less important in retail. Retail is one of the most yang activities. Its yang nature overrides problems that would be troublesome for a home. The main thing is a good location and good signage. The easier you make it for people to give you money, the more money they will give you. Money is the form of energy that fuels your store. Invite it graciously and welcome it with a smile.

Problematic Address

The words for "four" and "death" are similar in most Chinese dialects and in East Asian languages that have borrowed the words from Chinese. If you are not a native speaker of one of these languages, this connection has no meaning. The number four is fine in any part of an address, just as are any other digits. Numbers help us find locations via addresses; that is all.

The physical look of the numbers is what's important, and that can usually be adjusted after your purchase. If the numbers read down, that should be one of the very first changes you make.

Address numbers should never read going down. Example:

5
7
2

When you read the seven below the five, and the two below the seven, your vision goes down. This is not an auspicious direction to guide energy. Change the number to read horizontally or at an upward-tilting angle:

2
572   **7**
5

Troubled History

Try to find out whether any of the topics below relate to the building's history.

• **Death**—The seller is obligated to disclose if there has been a death in a building. If one has, it does not rule out buying the building. If the death was peaceful, usually all is well. If there was a violent or unusual death in the building, do a vibrational clearing. Any home or building benefits from having a clearing. Clearing is a very important part of moving into a space. Try to do it before moving your possessions into a new house. Clearing is essential for buildings with a violent death in their past, and highly recommended any time you move.

• **Divorce**—Some houses don't have good relationship energy. Relationships break up there, or somehow the occupants always remain single. Sometimes this is caused by a missing Relationship Area (page 10), a center bathroom (page 11), or features that portend disharmony (page 49). Sometimes the breakup was bound to happen anyway; feng shui certainly isn't the only factor influencing your life. But if a divorce happened in the home, remedy any of the aforementioned feng shui problems and do a clearing.

• **Disease**—Health problems are indicated by a center bathroom (page 11) and poison arrows (page 36). Poison arrows can be fixed, but a center bathroom is very bad feng shui. Don't get a home that has one. If prior occupants of the home had a history of health problems, do a clearing, and read *Feng Shui and Your Health* and *Feng Shui and Health* (see Recommended Reading, page 72).

• **Abuse**—any kind. You may have no way of knowing if abuse occurred in the home, and I think that's one of the best reasons to do a clearing any time you move. Abuse imprints a space with its vibration. Abuse is the opposite of gratitude. A space that shelters us is essential and something to be grateful for.

Baolin Wu is one of the greatest living feng shui masters. He says, "Children feel and see many things that adults cannot." His book, *Lighting the Eye of the Dragon* (see Recommended Reading), describes a specific technique of observing the behavior of a young child in a new space to determine if there are lingering vibrations.

Clearing

Clearing removes old, stuck vibrations from a place. You are clearing the air etherically.

Begin with cleaning the place thoroughly and letting fresh air circulate. Cleaning is an act of gratitude and in itself does most of the work of vibrationally clearing a place. Don't bring in electronically transmitted sound such as a radio or CDs. Do the work very consciously when cleaning a place for the first time. Especially pay attention to any place that is dank or dark.

After the house is thoroughly cleaned, walk around each room clockwise (turning left upon entering). Carry a lit stick of sage incense. (See Resources, page 136.) Sing, chant, or pray—peacefully but rather loudly. With your voice you are lovingly and authoritatively introducing yourself to the new home. The degree of authority in your voice matters. You are in charge now, and any old vibrations must leave. The importance of your voice—or friends' voices if others are with you—cannot be overstated. Singing bowls are a nice adjunct to clearing. When their tone vibrates through a space, it feels as if something etheric is happening.

Go *everywhere* in the home. Hand clapping and bell ringing are especially effective in dark, stagnant places. Clap your hands sharply, as if you were shooing a cat away. You'll need to safely put the incense down, or hand it to someone else, or make more than one trip throughout the place. See Recommended Reading for more on clearings.

There is the rather rare instance of "problem sellers"— when a seller seems determined to make your (and your agent's) life hell. You've got to hang in there if it's where you really want to live. And as soon as you take possession of the home, do an energetic clearing. I recently consulted at a home not far from where I live, and the sellers had been very problematic. The new owners did not feel comfortable in the house. Even if the "problem sellers" did not live in the residence, you should still do a clearing. Then you have a home that will be for *you* and not the previous owners. The memory of the painful transaction will fade more easily and naturally.

Floor Plans

When making the selection of a future home based primarily on seeing the floor plan, it's best to consider these common situations as feng shui **vetoes**. Keep looking at floor plans until you find houses without these problems. If you are planning or designing a home, here's the information you need *before* you start building:

- **Central bathrooms** are the most common reason to pass on a home.

- After that, look at the **two back corners**. If either of them is *missing* from the floor plan, don't get that home.

- If there's a **bathroom in the far-left corner** (Wealth Corner) of the floor plan, don't select that plan.

- **Stairs**

  - should not be spiral

  - should not be aimed directly at the door if they are visible from the door

  - should touch an outside wall somewhere

- **Triangular floor plans** should never be considered. Thankfully, they are rare.

Recommended Reading for Buyers

If you have time to read only one feng shui book, then the book you have in your hands now is the one I recommend the most. But if you have time to read two books on feng shui, make *Choose the Best House for You* by Elliot Jay Tanzer the second one you read. It's written for buyers and renters, as well as residents who aren't planning to move. It's a large-format book with an amazing number of illustrations.

If you like the straightforwardness of *Feng Shui for Real Estate,* you'll appreciate two of my earlier books, *Feng Shui Demystified* and *Bedroom Feng Shui.* The first book introduces feng shui and the bedroom book goes in-depth about the most important room in the home.

There are hundreds of books on feng shui in English. My web site, fungshway.com, reviews some of them. Two books that stand out for their completeness and clarity are *Feng Shui for Dummies* by David Daniel Kennedy and *Feng Shui House Book* by Gina Lazenby. The Kennedy book is the most complete I've seen. Lazenby uses color photographs to educate, whereas it seems they are often used by others just to raise the price of their book.

I practice and teach Form School feng shui. Compass School feng shui relies heavily on Chinese numerology and astrology. While I have no problem with those disciplines, I am not drawn to live my life by them. If they appeal to you, here are two fine books that are especially relevant for home buyers. *Buy Your Home Smarter with Feng Shui* by Holly Ziegler goes in-depth about your personal "lucky" direction and your personal "lucky" number. *Feng Shui Your Home* by Sarah Shurety has a chapter on Directionology—which compass direction to move toward during a specific year. It's an important aspect of Compass Feng Shui and has to do with what's called "the Grand Duke."

There are many books about vibrational clearing. One of the best is *Creating Sacred Space with Feng Shui* by Karen Kingston.

Lighting the Eye of the Dragon by Baolin Wu is quite traditional and has a unique method of judging the subtle energy of a potential home. *Feng Shui and Your Health* by Dr. Jes Lim is also very traditional and extraordinarily complete. *Electromagnetic Fields* by Blake Levitt is a wake-up call. It explains where EMFs occur and which illnesses may have a strong connection to them. *Feng Shui and Health* by Nancy SantoPietro is brilliant—a true masterpiece.

Especially if you are a first-time house buyer, you *must* read a book on house inspection. If the condition or durability of the home is deficient in any way, that affects the value, and you must know about it before you make the purchase. It should come as no surprise that the health of the physical body of your home is an overriding feng shui concern. A well-cared-for cottage has much better energy than a cheaply built McMansion. *The Complete House Inspection Book* by Don Fredriksson is written for buyers and I especially like the checklists. Another, more recent, book is also for buyers, *The Confident House Hunter: A Home Inspector's Tips for Finding Your Perfect House* by Dylan Chalk. There are several other books on home inspection—read at least one.

Checklist for Buyers
Free-Standing Houses

This checklist is available as a free PDF download through the publisher's website. Visit my site, fungshway.com, for the link, or go directly to the Watermark Publishing site at bookshawaii.net and search for this book.

If you mark "yes" for any of these seven items—**don't buy that home or live in that house**. These are **deal-breakers** that are almost never feasible to change.

YES	NO	SITUATION
		Does the landscape slope steeply down behind the house? Page 20
		Is the house exposed on a hilltop or along the edge of the ocean? Page 6
		Is the lot triangular? Page 6
		Do you suspect high electromagnetic fields? If so, measure them. Page 8
		Is the house under the low flight path of airplanes? Page 9
		Is either of the two back corners missing? Page 9
		Is the house an A-frame? Page 60

If you answer yes to any of the following questions, know that they are potentially deal-breakers. These problems would require significant interior remodeling to be feng shui acceptable. If you eliminate the problem, using only real cures, then these need not be deal-breakers. Read the referenced pages to see if the real cures will be feasible for you.

YES	NO	SITUATION
		Is there a center bathroom? Page 11
		Is there a bathroom in the far left corner (Wealth Corner)? Page 16
		Are there upward stairs in a direct line with the front door, visible from inside the front door? Page 18
		Is there a central spiral staircase? Page 26

Checklist for Buyers
Condominiums and Apartments

This checklist is available as a free PDF download through the publisher's website. Visit my site, fungshway.com, for the link, or go directly to the Watermark Publishing site at bookshawaii.net and search for this book.

If you mark "yes" for any of these seven items—**don't buy that condominium or live in that apartment.** These are **deal-breakers** that are almost never feasible to change.

YES	NO	SITUATION
		Do you suspect high electromagnetic fields? If so, measure them. Page 8
		Is the building under the low flight path of airplanes? Page 9
		Is either of the two back corners missing? Page 9
		Is there a center bathroom? Page 11
		Is there a bathroom in the far-left corner (Wealth Corner)? Page 16
		Are there upward stairs in a direct line with the front door, visible from inside the front door? Page 18
		Is there a spiral staircase? Page 26

The following questions describe situations that greatly disturb the energy of a home. If you answer "yes" for any of these, **you can do better** in selecting a home that retains and circulates energy.

YES	NO	SITUATION
		Is the unit directly next door to a cemetery, mortuary, police station, fire station, or church? Page 42
		Is the unit next to a very busy highway? Page 40
		Are there entire walls of floor-to-ceiling windows? Page 27
		Is there no door between the main bedroom and its bathroom? Page 37

PART TWO

FOR SELLERS

Advice for Sellers

Feng shui is popular today because it works. The results of feng shui amaze me. A seller's agent recently told me, "When the client follows your advice, the place sells within a half a day to a week. When they don't, it continues to sit on the market." The principles were formulated in ancient China but are adaptable to modern situations. You don't need to be a rocket scientist to use feng shui. Most of the principles relate to common sense.

The spaces and objects around us have symbolic meanings. With feng shui we interpret those symbols and manipulate the objects to achieve our goals. The goals in selling real estate are to do it quickly, harmoniously, and for the best price possible.

The concept of chi energy is fundamental in feng shui. Chi is simply another word for energy (including attentive energy). The words can be used interchangeably. When selling a property, it's vital that the property attracts and welcomes the chi, which is the potential buyer's attention.

Beauty attracts and unkempt clutter repels. Other things that attract chi energy are movement, light, sound, and fragrance. We notice these things, even subconsciously. When you're selling property, your job is to make it as attractive to people as possible. Use common sense and good taste to make your place look as nice as you can.

Because objects have meanings (real and symbolic), every object affects the flow of energy around it. Every person's life force and attention are energies as well, and they are affected by the objects around them. It's as if every object has a voice, a subconscious message. When someone is looking at a place to buy, they are hypersensitive to those voices. The whole house is saying, "Here's the kind of energy I attract" and "What you behold is what you will become." You have to rethink every detail of the home, inside and out. Try to see it through the eyes of a potential buyer. It can be helpful to visit some homes for sale that are in the same price range as yours. A home in good repair, clean, and orderly, is saying, "Life is easy here." If the home is dirty, crowded, and in poor repair, it's saying, "This, too, will be your life someday. You won't be able to keep up."

If you are occupying the place that is for sale, it is important that you completely adjust to the fact that you are moving. It is a place for sale more than it is your home. Making this mental adjustment will immeasurably strengthen the effect of any physical adjustments you make.

Feng Shui Staging

Staging Concept

The term *staging* in real estate means that the house has been decorated to look its best, regardless of how it looked before being listed for sale. It would be nice if all homes looked their best at all times, but that's not reality. Regardless of how your home looked before it was for sale, it needs to start looking perfect as soon as you've decided to sell it. Try not to stop at anything short of perfection.

Aiming for perfection can be frustrating and overwhelming for someone in a home that needs a lot of work. If you know you can't get it all done, just make sure it's *very clean* throughout, and then work primarily on the first impression. Try for simplicity and charm. Hopefully that will cause people (chi energy) to smile. Attracting chi energy is what selling is all about.

Yin and Yang

The concept of yin and yang is ancient. It became popular in China between 700 B.C. and 475 B.C. It has remained popular because it is a simple yet profound way of categorizing things. Things are either more yin or more yang.

A house is called a *yang dwelling*—a home for living bodies. A mausoleum (or tomb) is a *yin dwelling*—a home for dead bodies.

When selling a home, your goal is for something very yang to happen. You want the property to change title. You want money to change hands. You want movement, not stagnation. So, help it happen by emphasizing certain yang aspects or characteristics, such as cleanliness, simplicity, and adequate lighting.

Yang	Yin
Clean	Dirty
Uncluttered	Cluttered
Simple	Complex
Fast	Slow
Alive	Dead
Active	Passive
Spacious	Cozy
Light	Dark
Vertical	Horizontal
Awake	Asleep
Moving	Stagnant

Exterior

Curb Appeal

Unless you're selling a condominium, staging begins outside your house. First impressions are ninety percent of lasting impressions. It is often said that people decide whether or not to buy a house as soon as they see it. Then they spend the next twenty minutes or so finding things about the place to confirm their decision.

You know your exterior staging is good when people turn their heads as they go by your house and say, "Nice." You've invited positive chi energy. A house badly in need of a good paint job cannot attract good energy—it just can't.

Do not neglect the yard. If you have a lawn in front, it should be freshly mowed before any showings. Good landscaping is one of the best things you can do to enhance the value of your property—even more than adding a pool. I highly recommend that you incorporate some easy feng shui principles in your landscaping:

- Plant round (or rounded) leaf plants—and avoid sharp, spiky-leaf plants—along the street side and along the driveway or walkway. The rounded shape invites energy to roll in comfortably whereas sharp leaves are threatening to the entering energy.

- Put red (or a noticeable color) at the driveway or walkway entrance. It is the mouth of your property and you are giving it a touch of lipstick. People who use lipstick don't smear it all over their face. They just go for the lips. Bring appropriate attention to the mouth of your property. It doesn't have to be red, just noticeable. Your goal is to make heads turn toward your house.

• Do not let plants touch the house, not even their leaves. That would be stifling energy.

Sometimes there is a storm drain alongside (or in front of) the driveway. If the storm drain is quite noticeable, energy slips away before reaching the house. To remedy this, glue a tiny mirror to the bottom of the grate. The shiny part of the mirror should face down to symbolically reflect the drain away from anyone approaching the house.

Exterior of House

The whole area directly in front of a building is called the ming tang, or "bright hall." The area directly before the front door—the front porch, if there is one—is the most significant ming tang. A foyer, directly inside the front door, is also a ming tang.

The energetic purpose of the ming tang is to adjust the vibrations that enter your life. It greets energy, and it should offer a gracious and hospitable welcome. Keep the area simple so the energy flows unimpeded. Without sacrificing the landscape's charm, keep the front yard fairly simple, uncluttered, and well-tended. No clutter on the porch, no clutter in the foyer. Absolutely nothing should stand out and say, "Repair needed."

If the house needs painting, consider a shade of yellow. It makes people happy and feng shui considers it a "gathering color." More people will come, and they'll be smiling.

Nearby Buildings

There are concerns about nearby buildings if their use is related to death. Being right next door to any of these things is inauspicious and can hurt a sale:

- cemetery (symbolizes death)

- mortuary (symbolizes death)

- church (a problem if funerals are performed there)

- fire or police station (symbolizes emergency)

A neighboring building can also have a foreboding shape or size. Watch out for these things:

- tall, sharp shapes, such as a spire or pointed antenna (symbolizes a drawn sword)

- a next-door building whose height dwarfs your building

- the corner angle of a building aiming at your building (See Illustrations 41 and 42.)

- the gable end of a steep roof pointed toward your building

The last two situations are called poison arrows because harsh energy is aimed at your building. It subtly weakens the building without ever touching it.

Illustration 41 (left): Poison arrow created by neighboring building
Illustration 42 (right): Poison arrow from another house

In any of the above eight instances, use a mirror to reflect the nearby building away from you. It symbolically pushes away any restless or harsh energy. The mirror can be very small, less than one inch. (These are available in craft supply stores.) The mirror should be placed on your building in a discreet place, reflecting the other building.

You can use a small mirror to push away nearby energy that feels unfriendly in any way. It could be bad neighbors or an empty, littered lot.

If the home is not for sale, I sometimes recommend a bagua mirror. It is octagonal and has three lines, called trigrams, on each of its eight sides. In my experience, they are quite powerful and shouldn't be used indiscriminately. Don't use them on a place that is for sale. They look odd, and often cheap. They also signal that something is wrong.

Front Door

The formal front door is preeminently important. It is the mouth of the home. The front door should be very noticeable when the house is first seen. If the front door is around to the side or otherwise hidden, you may be greeting chi energy with a question mark: "Where's the door?" If the front door is easily seen, you don't have to do much more in this area—just the usual clean and uncluttered look.

If the front door is at all recessed, it should be appropriately emphasized. Don't use wind chimes. I often recommend them for residences, but almost never on a home for sale. They're too personal; not everyone likes them. A better solution is a plant in a glazed pot near the door, if there's plenty of room. The pot should be a very noticeable color so that even if the plant isn't flowering, the eye is still drawn to that area. When you draw the eye, you are drawing chi energy.

In regular residential consultations, I sometimes suggest that the front door be painted a noticeable color. I don't suggest the same thing when a home is for sale. A bright-colored pot is one thing, but a whole vividly colored door might put off some folks. Color preference is individual, and with dramatic colors even more so. As long as the door looks nice and the hinges don't squeak, it's enough for the sale. If the front door is truly hidden, off to the side or around back, make it obvious where to go. Use pathways that leave no doubt. Also use signage, such as a welcome sign near the path to the door.

When the home is for sale, don't display your name anywhere outside. It keeps you stuck there and hinders buyers from picturing themselves there. The address is sufficient without your name.

If there are stairs going up to the front door, they need to have risers connecting the treads. (See Illustration 43.) Without risers, the energy does not fully reach the front door. A lot of energy slides between the treads. It's usually easy to add risers to wooden stairs. If the stairs are made of concrete or metal, it may not be possible to add risers. In that case, all you can do is visually emphasize the door.

Illustration 43: Side view of stairs with both treads and risers (left); side view of stairs with no risers (right)

Doors to the home from other areas—such as the carport, garage, or side doors—are *somewhat* important. They need to be clean and uncluttered.

Interior

Your goal is to make viewers' jaws drop. You want beauty so stunning they nearly faint and quickly say, "I'll take it," or better yet, "I'll pay more." That goal is perhaps too high to achieve but keep aiming for it. It's now your job, and the payoff is huge. Take it at least as seriously as an eight-hour-a-day job.

The following list is somewhat long, but it's in order of priority. The most important topics are first.

Furniture

Of the various furniture scenarios, one of the worst is no furniture. It's a noticeably awkward yin/yang imbalance. Too yang to feel really comfortable, and too yin because the impression is "No life here—why live here?" The buyer is presented with questions everywhere, and that's never the best way to say hello to good chi energy. You are requiring the buyer to *imagine* living there, without actually *seeing* what it looks like to live there. Just because someone is a potential buyer doesn't mean they've got a great imagination. Your goal is to appeal to the broadest spectrum of people. When you limit your prospects to those who have good imaginations, you are limiting the amount of chi energy that your home can attract.

An empty house just says "empty." The symbolism of the objects in your home and their arrangement is crucial when it is for sale. Their subconscious message needs to be, "Those who live here are happy and successful, and if you live here, you will be too." An empty house misses the opportunity to deliver that powerful message to potential buyers. If the house is empty, it must be kept clean. You can also use the bagua (next chapter) in subtle but powerful ways.

When there is furniture, your job is to present an arrangement (with a limited number of decorative objects) that looks inevitable—as if angels dropped down out of heaven and put it there for you. Prospective buyers often wonder where to put the couch or bed. Show them a furniture arrangement that feels comfortable and flows well, even though they may not understand the considerations that went into the arrangement. If the arrangement looks clumsy, it says, "This home is hard to decorate."

The furniture should look inviting. Imagine a chair or couch to be a person. As you enter the room, they've either got their arms open to you or their back to you. Open arms are welcoming. If the back of a chair, and especially a couch, is first presented when entering a room, it symbolizes a chilly reception—a person with their back to the guests coming in. Try to arrange the seating so that you don't have to walk around it to sit in it. Make it easy to walk into the room.

Clutter

The only thing worse than no furniture is too much furniture, or too much stuff in general. The message is that the home is too small. Never ever give that message to potential buyers. If your home is crammed and cluttered, put this book down and start packing. Any time that you're not eating or sleeping, you need to be packing. Get help if necessary—friends, family, or professionals. It doesn't matter what you do with the packed boxes, as long as they are out of the living area. Hopefully they can go to off-site storage, but the boxes could also be put in the basement or garage if there is no alternative. A neat group of boxes that are labeled and ready for moving can say, "These folks are expecting a quick sale."

A clean and uncluttered look is often all it takes for a fast sale. Decide which items to leave on display—keeping in mind that *less is better*. Just leave the highest quality items. A well-made item lifts the vibrations around it. It makes you smile.

De-personalization

De-personalize the home by removing photos of yourself, family, and friends. Keeping them on display keeps you more firmly stuck in the house. You're moving, so pack them up. You want the buyers to easily picture their own family and friends in the space. Items that are particular to you or to your family's life or history should be packed away, such as photos, trophies, awards, diplomas, and coats of arms.

I recommend taking de-personalization a step further. Don't display artwork that shows people. You are trying to appeal to all races, so don't have artwork that shows only white people, for instance. The thing to remember is that your home is *for sale*. If a home is not for sale, this degree of de-personalization is not necessary. More pertinent information on artwork is on pages 122 and 124.

Avoid a look that is quirky or oddball—there should be no strange objects that need explanation. Having such items on display works against your purpose and is likely to slow the sale. Quirky artwork should be removed even if it is professionally made and expensive. Any obviously amateur artwork by non-famous artists should not be on display when showing a home to prospective buyers.

Remove any visible religious or political items or signs with words (such as quotes or affirmations). Everyone has their own beliefs, and you're not trying to convert anyone. You're just trying to sell the house.

No ashtrays should be seen. Even if they are clean, they can subconsciously tell the buyer to "sniff the drapes."

Color

Bold and dramatic colors can stop real estate sales. They're too in-your-face for something so decidedly personal as buying a home. Much of what attracts chi energy is vision related. If your eye gets a big dose of a color that you don't really care for, it does make an impression. You're not tempted to linger. Part of you consciously or subconsciously tries to block it out. Bold colors or murals on walls usually are painted over by the new owner. Save them the trouble. You'll have a faster sale.

Don't use over-the-top colors anywhere, inside or out, when a building is for sale. Inside a home, they're not a good idea any time. They're likely to bring too much drama into your life. The designer Clodagh says, "Kindergarten colors are hard to live with. Colors should not be intrusive. I prefer subtle colors, not-quite colors…" Leave drama for the soap operas. Off-white may seem boring, but it sure sells a lot of houses.

Architectural Detail

Most people experience architectural detail subconsciously but haven't trained themselves in seeing it consciously. Appropriately emphasize architectural detail when possible—perhaps simply by cleaning a complicated-but-grand stone fireplace or painting a built-in feature to match the color of something else in the room. Historic authenticity has a feeling to it that can never quite be reproduced. If your house is even twenty years old, it most likely has something about its design or detailing that dates it (in a good way). Don't carelessly erase that. Appropriately emphasized architectural features give a home an authentic charm that works wonders on potential buyers. They are literally charmed but may not know exactly why.

Emphasize architectural detail on the exterior as well. Paint is an efficient method. Maximize what is already there. The message is "smart" design. Your home will subtly say, "I'm intelligent."

Some homes have ill-designed add-ons. Your challenge is to make them seem logical and well designed. To do this, you might need a short, focused consultation with an interior decorator.

Dark Places

Any part of a building that seems unusually dark harbors stagnant energy. It can be a room, or part of a room, or most of a house. Lighten it with higher-wattage bulbs or lighter paint. Also try to bring fresh air to it. Use a fan if necessary, but put the fan away when the place is being shown.

If you do a vibrational clearing of the property (instructions for doing so are on page 69), pay special attention to dark places as well as low places, such as basements. That's where stagnant energy collects.

Long Hallways

Long, straight hallways cause energy to move quickly and become harsh. Think of a bullet guided by a long, straight rifle barrel. Slow the fast energy by using:

- carpet and/or rugs

- good lighting, preferably adjustable

- tactile art (art that invites touch); pictures without glass over them are preferable to those with glass in this instance.

Interior Bathroom

I discuss this topic at length in the "For Buyers" section of this book. If you have a bathroom that is not adjacent to an outside wall, it almost certainly will cause problems in your life. I often see this in homes that are hard to sell. You can't use most of the remedies I usually recommend because they look too strange in a home for sale. Instead, keep the door closed during showings. Use green or yellow as accent colors on items such as towels. If possible, put a mirror outside the bathroom so that it reflects energy away from the bathroom.

Drains

Water symbolizes money; therefore, drains represent money draining away. In a house for sale, de-emphasize drains appropriately. The most appropriate way to de-emphasize the largest drain is to keep the toilet lid down. That's what it's made for. Simply closing the toilet lid helps the vibration of any bathroom immeasurably. Lids that gently close themselves with a slight nudge are ideal—I'm glad they were invented.

Other drains are less important because they're smaller and less noticeable. A shower that has a curtain or doors can easily hide its drain. Just move the shower curtain or sliding door toward the drain side, so the drain isn't immediately seen. I recommend that the curtain or door be left somewhat open so that the room feels larger. If the shower has a hinged door, however, it should be closed during showings. Sink drains are the smallest and least important. They should look ready for daily use. That way you're not drawing undue attention to them.

There is a feng shui technique of using red thread to symbolize that a drain is cut off. The directions are on page 117.

Plants

Do not have dried plants in a house that is for sale. They are dead, and they symbolize death—the ultimate yin state. Emphasize yang in a place for sale with fresh flower arrangements or silk flowers. Fresh flowers are best but artificial plants are not a problem (and better than wilting or dead arrangements). They represent a living, growing plant. Use them to create beauty and enhance empty areas, taking care that you don't over-clutter the home. They must be clean. Take the time to arrange the leaves and try to imitate nature. The extra effort is worth it.

Real, healthy houseplants are ideal because they're actually alive. They say to buyers, "You can grow thriving houseplants here. You, too, can flourish."

Pets

If pets live in the house for sale, they and their smell and hair need to be gone any time the place is shown. Also remove their bed and waste box. That may sound harsh to owners of wonderful pets, but some people are allergic to certain animals. You shouldn't say no to those possible transactions. That's slamming the door in the face of chi energy. Just because someone has an allergy doesn't mean they aren't the perfect buyer. Ask your agent or friends to be very honest if they notice pet odor. You may be used to it.

There's no problem with having well-behaved pets outside the house during a showing.

Odors

The smell in a house should be fresh—not like animals and not like mildew. Unpleasant lingering odors draw the attention of buyers, and not in a good way. Do not use potpourri or air fresheners since some people are allergic to them. On the other hand, it's fine to have the light scent of freshly baked, delicious food. You'll probably make chi energy linger, perhaps hoping for some cake.

Repairing Broken Things

Broken things anywhere on your property work against your sale. Fix anything that could use any kind of repairing. Be sure to lubricate hinges. The energetic message of a broken object is "Not functioning correctly," and since you want the sale to "function correctly" you need to repair the broken objects, remove them, or do a symbolic cure.

Recently I consulted for an agent, meeting her at acreage that was for sale. It was obvious to me that the owner was under stress from preparing the large property for showings. On our way from one building to another we passed an unusual object and I asked, "What's that?" He said in an exasperated tone, "It's one of those everlasting pools, but it didn't work when I bought the place." I didn't say a word more—not wanting to add to that particular burden. Later, I told the agent (who is very reliable about using feng shui in properties she represents) to put a small dot of red paint on the pool in a hidden place and say out loud, "This pool is fixed. The red symbolizes a new beginning for this pool," or words to that effect.

Decorative Pillows

Decorative pillows (throw cushions) have no place in a home that's being offered for sale. Their purpose in decorating is to make a room seem cozy, which is yin. "Cozy" is a word used in real estate as a positive way of describing a space that might be perceived as *too small*. "Spacious" is a better way for a home to look when it's for sale. Remove extra cushions from couches, chairs, window seats, and beds. Use only the cushions that were made for the seating, and for beds just use the pillows that are necessary for comfortable sleep. And whatever you do, don't give your pillows/cushions a "karate chop" dent on top. Once again, it's too yin, and as a design look, it's dated.

Closets and Cupboards

Closets and cupboards should not be crammed full. They need to look spacious. Pack excess items and remove them from the living area. Keep closet doors closed during showings, even if the house is empty. It's a neater look—more yang.

Switch Plate Screws

Take the time to set all the grooves in the heads of the screws in the switch plate and electrical socket covers identically. If you set them vertically throughout the house, you tilt the scale a bit more in the yang direction because vertical is a more yang and active direction than horizontal. If all the screws are already nicely set horizontally, don't change them. The fact that they are all the same is the main thing. It simplifies the look, making it more yang. It also subtly says, "The last person to touch these was a professional," because they're often the only people who will set the screws identically. Buyers' eyes notice these details, even subliminally. Switch plate screws are especially important because they are usually closer to eye level than socket covers. If any of the paint on the screws is chipped, replace the screw—nylon screws are very good for this use.

The Bagua

The information given so far derives from the oldest and most practical branch of feng shui, the Form School, or Landform School. The bagua is a more recent refinement of feng shui and uses the old Chinese teaching of the Five Elements. These are the same Five Elements used in acupressure and acupuncture. The roots of the bagua go back to the concept of yin/yang and a very old Chinese book, the *I Ching* (or *Yi Ching*), an oracle dating back as far as the tenth century BC. A more in-depth discussion of the bagua is in my first book, *Feng Shui Demystified*, which has several chapters on it. I was skeptical when I first heard about the feng shui bagua, but I was also intrigued because it seemed as if you could play with it, like a game. That's how I deal with it, and the results continue to amaze me.

The bagua (or pakua) is a grid of nine spaces that lies over the floor plan of a house. You can also apply the bagua to the map of your property. In each case it is oriented by the entrance. The bagua grid divides your property into certain areas that represent aspects of life. (See Illustration 44. Illustration 45 shows the bagua as a rectangle.) The chart on page 106 briefly explains all the bagua areas. For selling property, we're mostly concerned with the three back areas: Fortunate Blessings (Wealth), Fame, and Relationships. It's the interior rear third of the house. The far corners of any space are the two "power" corners. When a person is in one of those corners (Wealth or Relationship) they can easily see all of the space, including the entrance. The Fame Area is the middle third of the back wall. All three areas must be clean and in good repair.

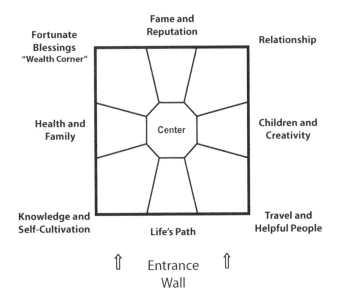

Illustration 44: The bagua map

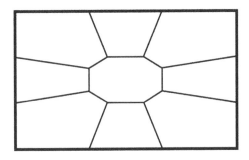

Illustration 45: Rectangular bagua map

Fortunate Blessings

This area includes the far-left corner and is often called the Wealth Corner. If there's no furniture, add something small and valuable, hidden from view. Perhaps use a coin or jewel. Possible hiding places are above the door or window trim, or under a carpet.

It is unlikely that someone would find and steal it, but I would hesitate to use something irreplaceable. Retrieve the object just before the deal closes.

I made this suggestion at one empty house that had been on the market for many months. The client said, "I have a ruby. Could I hide it under the corner of the carpet?" I replied, "If you're willing to put a ruby under the carpet, I can't think of anything more ideal." Solid offers started coming in the next week, and the house sold quickly.

A bathroom in the Wealth Corner symbolizes money draining away. It's the second worst place for a bathroom— the worst being the center. Keep the door closed and the toilet lid down. Make the bathroom simple but luxurious. An orchid or small flower arrangement is a good crowning touch.

Whatever room is located in the Wealth Corner needs to be ready for royalty. Make sure at least one of these colors is noticeable there: purple, blue, green, or red. Don't have an open trash can in a Wealth Corner. Relocate it or use a lidded trash can. The Wealth Corner is a good place for expensive objects and things made of precious materials such as gold. Put pictures of plants and/or water in this area. Water symbolizes wealth, and plants represent good fortune growing. Wood is the Element in this area, and Water nourishes Wood and helps it grow.

Sometimes the Wealth Corner is missing from a house. Put something noticeable or valuable in the exact place where the Wealth Corner would have been. (See Point A in Illustration 46.) You could bury a valuable coin in the ground there, then remove it just before closing the deal. When burying a coin, I suggest coating it in hot wax first to protect it. To remove the wax later, boil the coin in water.

Illustration 46: Remedy a missing Wealth Corner by placing something significant where the corner should be.

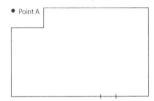

When the Wealth Corner is missing, put a small mirror on the inside of the home, on one or both of the walls tangent to the missing area. (See Illustration 47.) The mirror can be hidden behind curtains or a picture. Its purpose is to symbolically extend the house.

Illustration 47: Remedy a missing Wealth Corner by using mirrors.

Relationships

The Relationship Area is toward the far-right corner. The particular relationship we want to encourage now is the one between buyer and seller. Do so in these ways:

• Have one of these colors noticeable there: pink, red, yellow, or white.

• Put a pair of items in that area. They can be as large as two chairs or as small as two postage stamps. If the place is empty, you could tuck away two small coins. They don't have to be valuable, but they should be face to face. That says, "We're talking."

• Pottery is appropriate in this area because Earth is the Element here.

Certain things should not be in the Relationship Area and preferably not noticeable anywhere in a home for sale:

• Broken things—they say, "The deal is broken."

• A representation of a singular living being is inappropriate in this area. Be it a picture of one person, one dog, or one flower—it should not be alone. Two is the minimum beginning of a relationship. Groupings larger than two are also okay. It's better if the things are similar. They don't have to match perfectly, but it's fine if they do.

• Don't display artwork showing conflict, such as pictures of war scenes or ships in a storm.

• Don't have weapons or objects that could hurt someone, such as guns, swords, or knives.

If the Relationship Area is missing, put a mirror of any size on one or both of the inside walls tangent to the missing area. (See Illustration 48.)

Illustration 48: Remedy a missing Relationship Corner by using mirrors.

The purpose of the mirror is to represent a window. It is made of glass, like a windowpane. If you could put your hand through the "window" (the mirror and the wall behind it), your hand would be outside in the missing area. Decorators use large mirrors to enlarge a small room. Feng shui does exactly the same thing. If both the inside walls were a solid sheet of mirror, the area would not seem missing. Feng shui uses tiny mirrors when large mirrors are not appropriate. The mirror can be hidden behind a painting.

Outside the home, find the exact place where the apex of the missing Relationship Corner would have been. (See point A in Illustration 49.) Discreetly hide two small matching things there. They could be two coins face to face. Even though they aren't noticed, they symbolically complete the missing Relationship Area.

Illustration 49: Remedy a missing Relationship Corner by placing something significant where the corner should be.

Point A •

Fame

The back wall of a room is noticed first because it's directly in front as you enter. The middle third of the wall is in the Fame Area. Fire is the Element here. Put something here that has at least one of these characteristics:

- Denotes fame—use whatever you have. One client used a real signature of Queen Victoria. Another client had a large Coca Cola promotion displayed as pop art.

- Red—any shade of red except an earth tone like terracotta pottery. Good shades of red include bright red, pink, dusty rose, magenta, maroon, burgundy, violet, and even purple.

• Angular—the shape that symbolizes Fire is an angle. If the house is empty, you could cut a small red paper triangle and tuck it away in the Fame Area.

• Depicts an animal or is of animal origin, such as leather, bone, or feathers. Animals (including people) have "the fire of life" and represent Fire.

• Depicts plants or is of plant origin, such as wood, paper, or fabric (even synthetic fabric). All plants represent Wood, and Wood feeds Fire and makes it burn more brightly.

• Electrical—electricity is fiery, and electric objects enhance this area.

Don't keep water or a picture of water in the Fame Area. Water can extinguish Fire, so it is inappropriate there.

If the Fame Area is missing, use one, two, or three mirrors on any of the three interior walls that are tangent to the missing area. (See Illustration 50.)

Illustration 50: Use mirrors to remedy a missing Fame Area.

Bagua Chart

AREA (GUA)	ELEMENT	COLOR	SHAPE	ENHANCEMENTS
Life's Path	Water	Black and blue, especially dark blue	Free-form, amorphous	Perfect place for a fountain, fish tank, or a picture of flowing water; maps and globes
Knowledge	Earth	Brown, dark green, and dark blue	Horizontal, rectangular, square, or octagonal	Good place for books and learning tools, including TVs or computers; pictures of mentors
Health and Family	Wood	Green and blue	Vertical, rectangular, or square	Good place for plants/plant images, wooden furniture, and tall objects; pictures of ancestors
Fortunate Blessings or Wealth	Wood	Rich shades of purple, blue, green, and red	Vertical, rectangular, or square	Expensive items; living or artificial plants; fountain or picture of water; no open trash can
Fame	Fire	Red and purple	Angular, triangular, pointed, conical	Items related to fame—awards, diplomas; items representing animals or made from animals
Relationship	Earth	Pink, white, red, yellow, and warm brown	Horizontal, rectangular, square, or octagonal	Pairs and groupings of objects; no outstanding singular objects; preferably no TV
Children and Creativity	Metal	White and pastels	Circular, oval, or arched	Items relating to children, and/or creativity; items made of metal including metallic paint or fabric
Helpful People and Travel	Metal	Black, white, or gray	Circular, oval, or arched	Images of teachers or mentors—also a good place for affirmations
Center	Earth	Yellow, orange, brown, and earth tones	Horizontal, rectangular, square, or octagonal	No bathroom, ever! A good place for pottery or rugs. Try to keep this area open and traversable.

Special Situations

Commercial Property

Staging

Regardless of its location or purpose, commercial property for sale must be clean, neat, and in good repair. If the place needs a lot of work, either start immediately, or expect disappointing offers. The goal is to attract abundance, and there's only one way to do it: Make the place attractive! People are chi energy, and they like what looks good.

If businesses are currently occupying the property, they need to look prosperous. If that's a challenge, be creative.

Bagua

Put something valuable in the Wealth Corner (far left). It can be small. Put a pair of items in the Relationship Corner (far right). It can be two coins face to face. Put something red in the Fame Area (the back wall between the two previously mentioned corners).

Poison Arrows

If the place for sale has the corner of a nearby building pointing at it, use a small, discreet mirror to push it away. It's the same as in a residential situation. (See Illustration 51.)

If your building is dwarfed by a nearby larger building, put a concave mirror outside, facing the larger building. If a concave mirror calls attention to itself, don't use it. During the sale, it would draw attention to the problem. Instead, use a tiny, discreet, flat mirror.

Illustration 51: Use a mirror on your building to deflect a poison arrow aimed by a neighboring building.

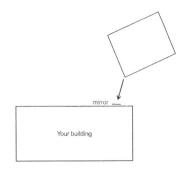

Raw Land

Staging

There's very little staging to be done for raw land. Keep it neat and litter-free, and make the entrance to the property noticeable and inviting.

Bagua

Using the bagua on raw land is also easy. Find the Wealth Corner and put something valuable there, perhaps a buried coin. It should be valuable enough that you wouldn't forget it or consider leaving it behind when the property sells.

Find the Relationship Corner and put a pair of items there. You could put two coins face to face in the ground.

Anywhere in the Fame Area, put something red. A red plant is fine.

The things that you put in the three bagua areas don't have to be noticeable, and only the item in the Wealth Corner needs to be valuable.

Poison Arrows

The only poison arrow to be concerned with on raw land is a nearby looming object. It would need to be close and foreboding to be a problem. Such instances are a bare lot next to a skyscraper, or land that borders a tall cliff.

The solution is to put a mirror at the edge of your property facing the foreboding object. It can be a small mirror. It reflects and pushes away the overly large object. This is one of the few instances where feng shui recommends using a concave mirror if possible. (See Illustration 52.) A concave mirror shows the object turned upside down and thereby makes it less important.

Illustration 52: Side view of a concave mirror

Pregnancy

If a pregnant woman is living in the home that is being sold, that's a *very* special situation. I've known it to speed up a sale and I've known it to stop a sale. This is an educated guess, but I think it has to do with where the baby wants to be born.

The first real estate consultation I had was for a couple in Marin County, California. The wife was pregnant, and I didn't think anything of it. I simply went through the house giving my recommendations. They reported back to me that that night (directly after the consultation) the mother-to-be had a very powerful and significant dream. (I didn't ask the specifics.) They then went shopping for the items that I'd recommended to help their home sell. When they arrived home from shopping, there was a couple standing in front of their house. The couple was interested in buying it, and the transaction was so quick and easy that my clients were able to return all the items that I'd suggested. It seems that the fact that they had committed to buying the items was enough to ensure the sale.

In studying feng shui, I have read that if a woman moves from one home to another while she's pregnant, then the child is more likely to have some "gypsy blood." In other words, it's likely to take longer for that child, when they grow up, to find a place they can really call home. That was very much the case in my life, so I asked my mother if she had moved homes while pregnant with me. She said, "Lord, yes! We moved from Colorado to New Mexico." And it wasn't done in a single move—there were at least three moves before getting to Fort Sumner where I was born. (And I am happy to be able to say I'm from the Land of Enchantment.)

I used that bit of personal knowledge when consulting for a pregnant woman on Hawaii Island. I'd seen the home when she married her husband and had just moved into his house, and then I had come again later when she was expecting their first child. Then I got a call from her when she was pregnant with their second child. They had decided to sell their home so they could move to the Northeast where she had relatives to help with their growing family. The house had been sitting on the market and just wouldn't sell, and she was getting antsy because she wanted to be near her relatives before giving birth. I boldly suggested that the child who was conceived on this island might want to have their first breath on this island. I told her the story that my mother told me about my family moving around while she was pregnant with me. My client said that made perfect sense to her (which I was relieved to hear). They took the house off the market until the birth, and then bingo, the place sold quickly.

Problematic Address

There is a concern about the number four (in an address) in certain feng shui books. The words for "four" and "death" are similar in most Chinese dialects and in East Asian languages that have borrowed the words from Chinese. If you are not a native speaker of one of these languages, this connection has no meaning. The issue will probably never come up unless the potential buyers are native speakers of one of those languages.

Troubled History

If there was a violent or accidental death in the building, do a vibrational clearing. Instructions are on page 69.

Any older building can have energy stuck in it. A vibrational clearing will help the stagnant energy move on and speed the sale.

Saint Joseph Statue

The reason I'm listing this last is because it has nothing to do with feng shui. The only reason I'm listing it at all is because I've never known it to fail since the very first time I mentioned the Saint Joseph statue to a seller in the San Francisco East Bay area.

She and her family were from India and they were going to be moving to a home they had already selected in Bakersfield. (I had the darnedest time trying to explain Saint Joseph's place in Christian iconography—he's the patron saint of home sellers and buyers—to my Sikh client.) She buried the statue upside-down in her front yard according to the directions that came with the small statue that she'd ordered online. Still the home did not sell, and they were getting anxious because they needed to close on the Bakersfield home.

Word finally came from an inspector that the Bakersfield home had severe structural damage, probably due to earthquakes. If my clients had sold their home sooner, they would have bought the new house without knowing of the severe problems. They selected a different new home and the old home then sold. The way I see it, St. Joseph protected them from a costly mistake.

I'm going to leave the intricacies of placing the statue to the internet and whatever source from which you might buy it. I will say that when using the St. Joseph statue to help sell a home, be sure to honor St. Joseph inside the home. A small, colorful prayer card to him would be appropriate if respectfully placed. It could be removed when the house is being shown, but afterward it should go back up.

Recommended Reading for Sellers

Dress Your House for Success by Martha Webb and Sarah Parsons Zackheim. This is a must-read for sellers. If you want to get top money, follow every word of their advice. The home should symbolically say, "The current residents are happy and successful." Webb and Zackheim guide you through the tiny details of the look that conveys that message.

Sell Your Home Faster with Feng Shui by Holly Ziegler is a very nice book. It includes plenty of general real estate information.

Many good books and audios cover the subjects of cleaning, de-cluttering, and organizing. Here are some of my favorites:

Getting Organized by Stephanie Winston. The audio is the thing to get; keep listening to it over and over.

Clear Your Clutter with Feng Shui by Karen Kingston. Don't settle for any other author. Kingston's the best.

Spring Cleaning and *Speed Cleaning* are the two best cleaning books that I know of. They're both by Jeff Campbell.

If you'd like to expand your feng shui knowledge, be aware that there are two main schools of feng shui, Compass and Form (or Landform). They use the bagua differently. A lot of feng shui books don't acknowledge the existence of the other school (whichever school that happens to be). That can cause confusion.

The Form School books I recommend are my own— *Feng Shui Demystified* and *Bedroom Feng Shui*. Also, *Feng Shui for Dummies* by David Daniel Kennedy is one of the most comprehensive I've seen.

Eva Wong is one of the greatest feng shui writers. She's top notch for both Landform and Compass. That's a rarity, and I recommend anything she's written.

Simon Brown has written many good feng shui books, but *Practical Feng Shui* is perhaps his best. Compass School is famous for being complicated, but he guides you right along.

Part Three

FOR AGENTS

Advice for Agents

Whether or not you are a licensed real estate agent, if you are involved professionally in the sale of real estate, apply the advice in this chapter to your own home. The energy of **your own home** matters to the sale. This advice is also good for buyers and sellers.

This chapter contains various tips to strengthen your position in transactions as well as advice to speed the transaction along. Apply them especially to **the home you are living in now,** because what's going on in your own home affects your business.

Money

Use your environment to signal that you are open to good fortune pouring in your direction. Money is a form of good fortune.

- Water symbolizes money. If possible, have a **fountain** outside your front door. The water must flow toward the home. It can be turned off at night, if desired, but should be on more than fifty percent of the time. It's best for it to run all the time. Don't use a fountain with a light bulb below the water. If you already have that kind of fountain, don't turn the light on. It symbolizes Fire under Water—a conflict.

If you cannot have a fountain outside your door, it can be inside the foyer. The water should flow toward the center of the home, not toward the front door.

- Repair any **dripping water** fixtures. They symbolize money dripping away, down the drain.

- Drains represent the ability of good fortune to drain away. Tie **red thread**, string or ribbon around any household drainpipes that you have access to. Red tape can also be used. This can be done discreetly, close to a wall, and often inside a cabinet. The symbolism is that the draining of money is cut off by the color red, which represents new blood—a fresh change from any old vibration.

- A large, **heavy object** (such as a flat barbell weight) can also be put directly under any and all drains (that you have access to) in the house. The heaviness symbolizes stillness and grounding and helps to counteract the movement of water leaving your home.

- Keep all **toilet lids down** when the toilet is not in use. It's the largest drain hole in the home and also the easiest one to hide. If you don't see the problem, it's as if it's not there.

• Put something red outside your **front door**. It can be a red doormat or a red tassel. I've seen marvelous red tassels. If you're in an apartment or a condo, that may be the only way to add red outside your front door. If space allows, it's nice to put a glazed red pot (with plant) outside your door. The red is like a stop sign saying, "Stop, Good Energy, come in here." If red isn't appropriate, use any noticeable color.

• If you have a **driveway**, put red on each side of the entrance. It's exactly the same dynamic as the red at the front door. Heads will turn—your driveway will be noticed. Energy comes in your direction because you've drawn visual attention. Red is best, but if it isn't appropriate in your situation, use any noticeable color.

• Hang a fairly large **mirror** on the wall in the **dining room**. Place it so the food is reflected in the mirror. This symbolically doubles your bounty. The mirror needs to be large because whether someone is standing or sitting they must be able to see their head reflected fully. A mirror must not "cut off" the top of your head in the reflection, and your throat should also be visible.

• The **stove** symbolizes money because it is used to prepare the bounty for the table. Keep the stove clean and in good working order. Cooking pots and pans must be kept orderly wherever they are stored. Do not store pots overhead because they are heavy and appear menacing, as if they could fall on your head.

Empowerment

The doorway to a room represents the future because that's where fresh energy arrives. When you spend significant time in a room, you are greatly empowered by being able to see the doorway. (See Illustration 53.) You are prepared for the future because you are looking toward the future. If you regularly sit or sleep with your back to the door, stop it right now. In real estate, you are involved with big financial transactions and don't want surprises. Use a mirror if the furniture can't be rearranged. Place the mirror so that you can easily see the doorway from your chair or bed. (See Illustration 54.)

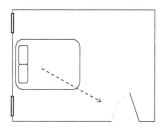

Illustration 53: An empowered bed position. You can easily see the doorway.

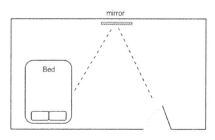

Illustration 54: A mirror placed as indicated allows you to see the door from the bed.

Seeing the door is also important when you're at the kitchen stove. Use a shiny, dome-shaped tea kettle or a convex mirror if there is no other option. There are no symbolic fixes—you've got to really change the dynamic of not seeing toward the door. The most crucial places, ranked by importance, are:

- bed
- desk
- stove
- lounge chair
- your dining place

In all of the above places, try to position a solid wall behind your back—not a window, and not the openness of the room. The wall symbolizes *backing*—decisions that are backed up, and financial backing.

An entire house is disempowered if the land behind it slopes down—especially if it slopes down steeply. The house symbolically lacks support or backing. This is also true of any home with an in-ground swimming pool directly behind the house. (Pools are further discussed on page 44.) There are several remedies for this (starting on page 20), but the most feasible one is to hang a mountain picture on the back wall inside the house. This symbolically puts a mountain behind the home. A mountain image behind your desk chair is also a good idea because it says that you've got the backing to do your business.

Relationships

The important relationship in a real estate transaction is between buyer and seller. You want people to be amicable and for things to go smoothly, but there are certain household features in your home that have the potential to symbolically say "argument." These general feng shui tips promote harmony and thereby speed the transaction:

- In the **kitchen**, the stove represents Fire. The refrigerator and sink represent Water. A severe conflict is symbolized if Fire is immediately next to Water or directly across from it. If the stove (oven or rangetop) is directly across from the refrigerator or sink, it's fairly easy to deploy a symbolic remedy. Hang a crystal from the ceiling midway between the two appliances to symbolize dispersion. A more discreet remedy is to put a red line between the two opposing elements. The red line can be as invisible as a thread glued to the bottom of a rug. If it fits your décor, I've seen kitchen rugs with a red line designed into the pattern. No matter what, the red line must be parallel to the appliances, symbolically separating them. It's often possible to put a red string or red tape under the countertop, such as between the front edge of the sink and the lip of the counter. Open the cabinet below the sink (or rangetop) to access the underside of the countertop.

  If the refrigerator is *right* next to the stovetop, it's poor design and bad feng shui. I've even seen scorch marks on the side of the refrigerator. There is precious little space to work with. Use a crystal as a symbolic remedy. Put the crystal directly above the small gap between the two appliances to disperse their conflicting energies. It can also be tucked in a cabinet above the refrigerator or stove. Place it as close to the gap as possible.

• A support **pole** (or column) in the middle of a room suggests disagreement. One eye sees on one side, and the other eye sees on the other side: "Here's how I see things." "Oh, no, I see things differently." Remedy this with a large plant or large furniture placed next to the pole. This causes the pole to blend with other objects and become less important. A pole at the edge of a space, such as a porch, is not a problem.

• The **artwork** in your home can either say, "We're together on this deal," or not. Artwork that says "together" has more than one living being depicted. The living beings can be plants, people, or animals. If none of those is in the artwork, it probably has a neutral effect on the sale. Don't have a lot of singular images in your home. It takes at least two to make a deal.

• If the **knobs** or handles of two different doors can touch each other, they are referred to as "clashing knobs." They represent two heads butting against each other. Hang a red tassel or thread from each knob that can touch another knob. The red supersedes the old dynamic by establishing a "new blood foundation." It can be any shade of red.

• **Stripes** can say argument, especially if they are bold stripes. One stripe represents one person's opinion. The next stripe is someone else's opinion. They're separate—they're not blending. Replace or de-emphasize boldly striped fabric.

• **Square windows** aren't too common, but they portend conflict. Use window treatments to make them look less square.

• Don't keep open **knife blades** on display in the kitchen. They can symbolize conflict and should be de-emphasized during the sale. Put them in a drawer or container that hides the blades.

• If a room has **two couches** that directly face each other, they symbolize "opposite points of view." Change the furniture arrangement, if possible. If not, put a cut crystal object on the coffee table between them. Its facets break up and disperse the two conflicting energies. The crystal object can be a paperweight, vase, candy dish, bowl, decanter, or similar item. It needs to be clear and faceted.

• Don't display anything that is obviously **broken**. An obviously damaged object boldly says, "broken." You don't want the sale to break off or fall through. Repaired things are not a problem.

Clarity

May your decisions be powerful, and may you have clear thinking in making those decisions. These tips help promote clear thinking.

- The **windows** of your home represent your eyes. Clean windows (and screens) symbolize seeing clearly. My first recommendation to anyone making important decisions is: "Clean your windows."

- Don't display **art** that depicts a human body without the head. (It says, "No thinking here.") Also, if it shows missing limbs, it's a problem. ("Can't get much done.") Such art may also be bad for your health.

One of my clients had a beautifully carved wooden torso of a human body on their coffee table. All aspects of his life were stagnant, his financial decisions had proven to be poor, and he was in bad health. When I explained the symbolism of the sculpture, he said, "I can return that to the gallery—they'll be glad to get it back." Of course, it isn't always that easy to part with an object, but if the artwork involves an incomplete body, it needs to go.

- A **mirror** in the home that doesn't show your head fully is a major problem. It cuts off your "thinker" and damages your decision-making ability. It's also bad for your health. Preferably, you should be able to see at least eight inches above your head in a mirror. That space represents your potential, your room to grow. Seeing it reflected makes your potential more easily attainable. Hang mirrors to properly reflect the adults in the home. Children are not impacted, unless the mirrors are in rooms solely for their use.

Mirror tiles are also a problem because they show your image broken up and suggest chaotic thinking. Smoked glass mirrors indicate dull thinking, as do mirrors with bad silvering. If a problem mirror cannot be replaced, at least cover it during the sale.

Achievement

Feng shui aids in achieving goals. These tips will help chi energy reach you. They will also alert you to potential obstacles.

- A **bare glass edge** (of a table or shelf) symbolically cuts you off from reaching your potential. Heed this warning! It is quite serious. If there is a bare glass edge that extends and is in a prominent location it is important to deal with it. It may look stylish, but it's not doing you any good and never will. **Cover it** or **get rid of it**. Please don't fall in love with your furniture. Save that emotion for things that can love you in return—family, friends, and pets. Furniture is replaceable.

There are three other options. You can put a rim around the bare glass edge. I've seen this done well using bamboo. Or you can use extremely thick glass—at least two-and-one-half inches thick, and preferably thicker. The edge should be frosted, not clear. Be aware, thick glass can be very heavy.

The third option will only work on somewhat thin glass, such as a glass shelf or some glass desktops—glass that is not over one-quarter-inch thick. Brandsport (see Sources) offers a plastic molding, which is generally used to keep car doors from touching things when they are opening. Be sure to ask for the *L-shaped molding*. They can send you a card with samples of dark green colors that will exactly match the color of glass edges. A thick glass dining table is too thick for this particular plastic molding.

Glass surfaces are not a problem if the edge isn't visible. If the edge is visible but doesn't extend beyond the edge of an underlying base or tabletop, it is also not a problem.

Glass surfaces that are tucked away in a corner and rather hidden by other furniture are not a severe problem. Glass shelves inside a cabinet with closeable doors are also not a severe problem, even if the doors are glass. If any side (or sides) of a glass table or shelf is directly against a wall, that side (or sides) is not a problem and does not need to be covered unless you want to.

- Certain situations represent **opportunities slipping away**. The front door is the symbolic portal of opportunities. The door must be able to open fully—not blocked by furniture or other objects. If there are stairs leading to the front door, they must not be open riser. (See Illustration 55.) Open-riser stairs allow most of the energy to slip away before reaching the front door. Install something vertical (wood or oilcloth) to connect the stair treads so you can't see through the stairs. (See Illustration 56.)

Illustration 55 (left): Side view of stairs with no risers
Illustration 56: Side view of stairs with treads and risers

The relationship of the front door to certain interior features can bode ill for opportunities. Here are five of the most problematic situations. They all involve something inside in a *direct* line with the front door and immediately visible from the door.

- A window or door on the back wall, in line with the front door. Energy zooms through quickly in a straight line and leaves too soon. The best solution is to put sheer curtains over the window, or keep the back door closed. You could also hang a crystal between the front door and the back window to disperse the energy. A third option is to put a mirror (any size) next to the back door or window. The mirror symbolically reflects the energy back into the house.

• Upward stairs within twelve feet of the front door. If the bottom of the stairs is in a direct line with the front door, the energy rolls back out the front door. A container (basket or umbrella stand) near the door will symbolically catch the energy. A mirror next to and on the same wall as the door reflects the energy back into the house. A crystal (or even a wind chime) hung between the stairs and the door disperses the energy. Hanging a bagua mirror over the front door on the inside is also a cure.

• A mirror on the wall opposite the door and within about ten feet of the door. This pushes energy out of the house immediately. Remove the mirror and hang artwork with perspective—a picture that shows a distant scene. It will make a small foyer seem more open.

• An open fireplace in a direct line with the front door. This offers chi the opportunity to immediately go up and out the chimney. Put a screen or plant arrangement in front of the firebox (the cavity where wood is burned).

• An open toilet easily visible from the front door represents flushed opportunities. Keep the toilet lid down when it's not in use and keep the bathroom door closed. I highly recommend toilet lids that gently close themselves.

• Wherever **shoes** are stored together in the home, place them in the same direction. They represent getting someplace—achievement. You're not going to get very far with your feet going in opposite directions, so don't leave your shoes that way. Shoes in one closet don't have to face the same direction as shoes in another closet. Shoes on one side of a large closet don't have to face the same direction as shoes on the other side of the closet.

• Transactions can mire for unexpected reasons. These are things that can slow you down because they represent **stagnation**:

  • Clocks that don't keep the correct time. Repair them, put them away, or get rid of them. Set all clocks to the same time.

  • Dried plants—they're dead. If you've had them for more than three months, let them go back to the earth.

  • Holiday decorations left on display long past the holiday.

  • Unused rooms—their stagnant energy affects the entire house. Make them feel fresher and more used. Leave their doors open. Open the windows occasionally. Put a low-wattage light on a timer in there. Consistently dark places anywhere in a home hold stagnant energy. Give them light and fresh air. Use a fan if necessary.

  • Faded pictures. Replace them or put them away.

  • Anything dusty or dirty. Be sure to remove cobwebs in high corners.

  • Clutter—it stops everything! Hopefully this is not a problem in your home. If it is, you *must* deal with it. Pack up what isn't being used. Label and date the boxes. The label on a box is sometimes the key difference between organization and clutter. If you need to de-clutter a large area:

    • Start near doorways. This is so fresh energy can easily flow in. It will greatly help you continue to de-clutter.

• Then de-clutter the center of the area. It is the heart of the space and greatly benefits from openness.

• The corners are next. Energy can stagnate in any corner that isn't well used.

• The rest of the space should be easy. You've got good energetic support to finish de-cluttering.

See Recommended Reading on page 113 for more de-cluttering encouragement.

Part Four

RESOURCES

Glossary

BAGUA MIRROR

A mirror with an octagonal (eight-sided) frame, with the *I Ching* trigrams around the eight sides. If it doesn't have the trigrams, it's just an octagonal mirror and not a bagua mirror. A mirror with the Chinese zodiac animals around it is also not a bagua mirror. For more information about the trigram arrangement in the bagua, read the yin/yang chapter in *Feng Shui: A Complete Guide* by Richard Craze. It's an extraordinarily lucid explanation.

Bagua mirrors represent good order and are considered powerful. Don't use a bagua mirror unless you need it. It shouldn't be used indiscriminately to "bring in good energy." It is a mirror; it reflects away. They are primarily for outside use and almost never appropriate inside, except for very onerous situations. Three such interior uses are described in the "For Buyers" section of this book under The Most Profound Problems (begins on page 5): Central Bathroom, Wealth Corner Bathroom, and Stairs in Line with Front Door.

Bagua mirrors are available online, or at Chinese drygoods stores. The mirror may have a blue-tinted plastic film sticking to the glass when you buy it. The film protects the glass before purchase. Remove that film before using the mirror; otherwise, it won't be very effective.

BULLNOSE CORNERS

These are pre-molded drywall beads that form a radius instead of making a sharp right angle. They are applied after the Sheetrock but before the mudding. They can also be installed at any time, although it's messy. Search under "drywall supplies."

CHI

Pronounced *chee*. Any form of energy.

CONCAVE MIRROR

This mirror curves inward, "caves in."
It enlarges a very close object but inverts a
distant object. Inverting the distant object
makes it less important. Use a concave mirror
outside when an overscale object (cliff or
skyscraper) dwarfs your building. Concave
mirrors absorb harmful energy.

CONVEX MIRROR

This mirror curves outward. It reflects
and disperses energy from many directions.
They're available where auto supplies are sold.

CRYSTAL

The best crystals for feng shui purposes are clear,
not tinted or iridescent in any way. The crystal may be
manufactured "lead-glass crystal," or natural, "from-the-
earth" crystal. Clear crystals are preferred because they make
the best rainbows in sunlight. Rainbows are formed when
light is dispersed into bands of color. That's why crystals
symbolize dispersion.

You may use cut crystal objects such as vases or bowls.
The best shapes for crystals that hang are disco ball or
octagonal. The octagon is preferred where sunlight can reach
it because it makes the largest and most distinct rainbows.
Lead crystal is softer than regular glass because it has a higher
lead content. If it bumps regular glass, it will easily chip.

If a natural crystal is used, it should be clear or have
rainbow rutilations.

ELEMENTS

There are five Elements according to Taoism: Water, Wood, Fire, Metal, and Earth. The word Element here has nothing to do with the periodic table of elements of Western science. In Taoism they refer to *archetypal energies.* Everything in the Universe is considered to be an expression of one of the Elements.

MIRROR, SMALL FLAT

These are the mirrors that I use the most. They are available at craft supply stores. Some are quite tiny and can be used discreetly. Any flat mirror reflects energy directly back.

See also *Concave Mirror, Convex Mirror.*

POISON ARROW

This (malevolent) chi energy is sometimes called sha chi or shar chi. It is chi energy that has encountered something in the environment that speeds it up or causes a harshness to develop. See Poison Arrows, pages 31 and 36.

REMEDY

Sometimes called a solution, cure, fix, or adjustment. It's whatever feng shui can offer to help the situation. A remedy can be real or symbolic. A real remedy is a physical change that eliminates the problem. Ideally, the problem vanishes.

A symbolic remedy is a symbol of your intention. You can make that symbol more powerful by saying out loud why you're doing it. You only need to say it once, at the moment when you do the remedy.

A hidden remedy works almost as well as a visible remedy. You can hide mirrors behind pictures or put crystals in boxes. As long as it stays there, it's working for you. You may use more than one remedy.

Wind Catcher

A wind catcher is a decorative item that moves in the wind but is silent. Whirligigs, windsocks, and banners are examples. Avoid the kind that point downward.

Wind Chime

A wind chime is a symbol of energy dispersed. It can be used instead of a hanging crystal in any of the remedies. Unless they are small, they can look awkward indoors. See page 136 for a source of very small wind chimes. If a wind chime is heard, you must like the sound, or replace the wind chime. A wind chime symbolizes dispersion because it takes the wind energy and disperses it into musical notes.

Yin/Yang

These are fundamental categories of classifying all things and energies in the Universe. Nothing is totally yin or yang, but on a sliding scale between yin and yang. See the list of yin/yang energies on page 83.

Retail Sources

AlphaLab, 800-658-7030, trifield.com

They sell gaussmeters for measuring EMFs—
electromagnetic radiation.

Brandsport, 541-341-6555 or 877-341-6555, brandsport.com

Be sure to ask for the **L-shaped molding**, which is
suitable for bare glass edges. *Don't* get the U-shaped molding,
which is *only* for car doors. They have a huge selection of
colors—every color that cars come in. Most people opt for a
dark green, but if the supports of the glass table are chrome,
then you might want to use a metallic silver molding to
match. This particular molding won't work on glass thicker
than one-quarter inch. The molding is flexible and will work
around curves. It has an easy peel-and-stick adhesive.

Karizma, 415-861-4515, karizma94114@gmail.com

They are an excellent source for **tiny wind chimes**.
They also have a good selection of **crystals** at decent
prices. They are a good place to get the best clear octagonal
crystals—the kind I particularly recommend have very few
facets and therefore make the largest rainbows. They are best
for windows and skylights where the sun actually reaches the
crystal. Karizma also has disco ball–shaped crystals.

This store also has **bagua mirrors** with convex,
concave, or flat mirrors. It can sometimes be hard to find flat
bagua mirrors. It can also be hard to find bagua mirrors that

are tasteful, but Karizma has some made of natural wood as well as the more traditional colorful bagua mirrors.

Juniper Ridge, 800-205-9499, juniperridge.com

A source of **sage bundles** as well as excellent **sage incense** for clearing, which is also called smudging.

Glenview Products, glenviewproducts.com.au

This company has an amazing variety of **weathervanes**—a veritable wonderland. I especially like that they have lots of bird weathervanes that don't look like they have a vertical spear through them. And they have plenty of weathervanes that don't say "singular" because there's more than one animal depicted.

Index

Bold page numbers refer to the most complete information on the topic. The books and authors in Recommended Reading are not included in the index.

Buyers' information is from page 1 to 77.

Sellers' information is from pages 79 to 114.

Agents' information is from pages 115 to 130.

About the Author

Clear Englebert is in his third decade as a feng shui consultant for the owners and tenants of thousands of homes, businesses, offices, and public buildings. He has witnessed transformations in the lives of his clients through the application of feng shui principles. Clear views feng shui as an interpretative language of visual symbols, avoiding superstition and consumerism in his practice.

In 2000, his first book, *Feng Shui Demystified*, was published by The Crossing Press of California, followed by *Bedroom Feng Shui* the next year. In 2008, his first Hawai'i book, *Feng Shui for Hawai'i*, was published by Watermark Publishing of Honolulu; the companion volume, *Feng Shui for Hawai'i Gardens* followed in 2012. In 2013, Clear self-published *Feng Shui for Retail Stores*, drawing on his five decades of retail experience, primarily in bookstores. In 2015, Watermark published *Feng Shui for Love and Money*, focused on the two main reasons why people first explore feng shui. Clear's books have been translated into four languages including Spanish, Japanese, German, and Portuguese.

Clear is at work on his next books, *Feng Shui Outside*, *Feng Shui with House Plants*, and *Feng Shui for Collectors*, in that order. Additional resources, including videos and book reviews, are available at his website, fungshway.com, and at his blog, clearenglebert.wordpress.com.

Made in the USA
Monee, IL
13 March 2024

54965097R00089